Goethe's *Faust*

Marie-Louise von Franz, Honorary Patron

**Studies in Jungian Psychology
by Jungian Analysts**

Daryl Sharp, General Editor

Goethe's *Faust*

Notes for a
Jungian Commentary

EDWARD F. EDINGER

Also by Edward F. Edinger in this series:
The Creation of Consciousness (#14, 1984)
Encounter with the Self (#22, 1986)
The Bible and the Psyche (#24, 1986)
The Christian Archetype (#28, 1987)

Canadian Cataloguing in Publication Data

Edinger, Edward F. (Edward Ferdinand), 1922-
    Goethe's Faust

(Studies in Jungian psychology by Jungian analysts; 43)

Bibliography: p.
Includes bibliographical references.

ISBN 0-919123-44-9

1. Goethe, Johann Wolfgang von, 1749-1832. Faust.
2. Goethe, Johann Wolfgang von, 1749-1832 — Symbolism.
3. Psychoanalysis.   4. Jung, C.G. (Carl Gustav), 1875-1961.
I. Title.   II. Series.

PT1930.E35 1990   832'.6   C90-093300-3

INNER CITY BOOKS
Box 1271, Station Q, Toronto, Canada M4T 2P4
Telephone (416) 927-0355

Honorary Patron: Marie-Louise von Franz.
Publisher and General Editor: Daryl Sharp.
Senior Editor: Victoria Cowan.

INNER CITY BOOKS was founded in 1980 to promote the
understanding and practical application of the work of C.G. Jung.

Cover: Rembrandt, "Faust in His Study Watching a Magic Disc."
    Etching, 1652. (National Gallery of Art, Rosenwald Collection)

Index by Daryl Sharp

Printed and bound in Canada by
University of Toronto Press Incorporated

Contents

See final page for descriptions of other Inner City Books

Faust *is the most recent pillar in that bridge of the spirit which
spans the morass of world history. . . . It seems to me
that we cannot meditate enough about* Faust, *for many of the
mysteries of the second part are still unfathomed.*
Faust *is not of this world and therefore
it transports you; it is as much the future as
the past and therefore the most living present.*

—C.G. Jung, *Letters.*

Preface

Goethe's *Faust* is a "document of the soul" of major importance for the psychological understanding of modern man. It is perhaps the central "collective dream" of the Western psyche during the final quarter of the Christian eon. *Faust* can be understood on many levels. It is a picture of modern man, a symbolic description of a depth analysis and the "final summit" of alchemy. *Faust* was Jung's life-long companion. He identified profoundly with Faust and took Faust's fate upon himself, thus providing a paradigm for others who belong to the Jungian eon.

A Jungian commentary on *Faust* is a "Faustian" enterprise that remains for the future. I offer these notes as a beginning.

A Note on English Translations

There is no satisfactory English translation of *Faust*. For clarity and general accessibility the best is Barker Fairley's prose translation which however occasionally lapses into paraphrase. For Part I only I like Peter Salm's unrhymed verse translation with the German on facing pages. Norton's Critical Edition with verse translation by Walter Arndt and copious explanatory notes by Cyril Hamlin is indispensable for any serious student. Philip Wayne's verse translation of Parts I and II in two volumes by Penguin is tolerable but not always true to Goethe's imagery. Louis MacNeice's verse version is the most poetic of all but has the fatal defect of being only an abridgement. George Madison Priest's verse translation is quite good but, unfortunately, is currently out of print.

Philemonis sacrum
Fausti poenitentia.

Jan. 1959.

C. G. Jung

Inscription carved by Jung over the entrance to his Bollingen tower:
Philemonis Sacrum—Fausti Poenitentia
(Shrine of Philemon—Repentance of Faust).

1
Introduction

Jung has demonstrated in *Aion* that the Christian eon is characterized by a process of enantiodromia[1] in which the figure of Christ is replaced by Antichrist.

> The dechristianization of our world, the Luciferian development of science and technology, and the frightful material and moral destruction left behind by the second World War have been compared more than once with the *eschatological* events foretold in the New Testament. These, as we know, are concerned with the coming of the Antichrist. . . . The Apocalypse is full of expectations of terrible things that will take place at the end of time, before the marriage of the Lamb. This shows plainly that the *anima christiana* has a sure knowledge not only of the existence of an adversary but also of his future usurpation of power.[2]

According to astrological symbolism the second fish in the constellation Pisces, associated with Antichrist, comes to the fore in the sixteenth century, coinciding roughly with the Renaissance, the Reformation and the Scientific Revolution.[3] It is highly relevant that the Faust legend began at the same time, gathering around an actual historical personage, Dr. John Faustus, who lived from approximately 1480 to 1540. Contemporary with Dr. Faustus were: Leonardo (1452-1519), Columbus (1451-1506), Machiavelli (1469-1527), Erasmus (ca. 1466-1536), Copernicus (1473-1543), Luther (1483-1546), Paracelsus (1493-1541), Vesalius (1514-1564).

---

[1] Running counter to. "I use the term enantiodromia for the emergence of the unconscious opposite in the course of time." (Jung, *Psychological Types,* CW 6, par. 709; CW refers throughout to *The Collected Works of C.G. Jung)*

[2] *Aion,* CW 9ii, par. 68.

[3] Ibid., par. 149.

The Faust legend is a corollary to the coming of Antichrist. In the sixteenth century the God-image fell out of heaven (metaphysical projection) and landed in the human psyche. In the course of this transition from heaven to earth it undergoes an enantiodromia from Christ to Antichrist. This event paves the way for Faust's encounter with Mephistopheles. The happening was predicted long ago in Revelation 12:12: "Woe to the inhabiters of the earth and of the sea! for the devil is come down unto you, having great wrath, because he knoweth that he hath but a short time."[4]

Of course the artists, scholars, explorers, reformers and scientists of the sixteenth century did not consider their activities as devilish. They were all good Christians, they thought, who were excited by the expansion of human knowledge and energy. But things looked different from the standpoint of the unconscious which, like a compensating dream, generated the Faust legend.

During the past 500 years the Faust legend has been told again and again in poetry, prose and music. E. M. Butler's *The Fortunes of Faust* describes fifty different versions. Of all of these the most notable is Goethe's *Faust* (Part I, 1808; Part II, 1832), which he worked on throughout his long life.

Goethe's *Faust* was profoundly significant to Jung. In his autobiography he tells us,

[I] realised with something of a shock [that *Faust*] meant more to me than my beloved Gospel according to St. John. There was something in *Faust* that worked directly on my feelings.[5]

And again,

In my youth (around 1890) I was unconsciously caught up by this spirit of the age, and had no methods at hand for extricating myself from it. *Faust* struck a chord in me and pierced me through in a way that I could not but regard as personal. Most of all, it awakened in me the problem of opposites, of good and evil, of mind and matter, of light and darkness. Faust, the inept, purblind philosopher, en-

---

[4] Biblical quotations are from the Authorized (King James) Version.

counters the dark side of his being, his sinister shadow, Mephistoph-eles, who in spite of his negating disposition represents the true spirit of life as against the arid scholar who hovers on the brink of suicide. My own inner contradictions appeared here in dramatized form; Goethe had written virtually a basic outline and pattern of my own conflicts and solutions. The dichotomy of Faust-Mephistoph-eles came together within myself into a single person, and I was that person. In other words, I was directly struck, and recognized that this was my fate. Hence, all the crises of the drama affected me person-ally; at one point I had passionately to agree, at another to oppose. No solution could be a matter of indifference to me. Later I con-sciously linked my work to what Faust had passed over: respect for the eternal rights of man, recognition of "the ancient," and the conti-nuity of culture and intellectual history.[6]

As for Jung perhaps also for others, Goethe's *Faust* may be a gateway leading beyond the Christian eon.

---

[5] *Memories, Dreams, Reflections,* p. 87.
[6] Ibid., p. 235.

2
Overture

Goethe's *Faust* is a great enterprise in active imagination.[1] It begins with a "Dedication."

> You shifting figures *[Gestalten]*, I remember seeing you dimly long ago, and now I find you coming back again. I wonder should I try to hold onto you this time. Have I the inclination, have I the heart for it? You draw closer out of the mist. Very well then, have your way. The magic breeze that floats along with you fills me with youthful excitement.[2]

Memories of the past emerge, "early love, early friends" and tears and pain "that life should be so wayward." Then comes the will to proceed.

> And a great desire seizes me—a desire I have not felt for years—to return to this solemn realm of the spirit *[stillen, ernsten Geist-erreich]*. My song resumes hesitantly, insecurely, like an Aeolian harp. I am shaken through and through. The tears come freely and my heart is softened. All my world now seems far away, and what was lost has become real and immediate *[Wirklichkeit]*.

Like Faust's opening himself to the encounter with Mephistopheles, Goethe submits himself to a confrontation with the autonomous psyche.

The active imagination begins with the "Prelude on the Stage," a three-way conversation among the director, the poet and the clown, each expressing a different approach and intention concerning the staging of the drama. It is as though the effort to make the *Geister-reich* manifest requires an encounter with the number three, the

---

[1] A technique for encounter and dialogue with the unconscious. See Jung, *Mysterium Coniunctionis,* CW 14, pars. 752 ff.

[2] Unless otherwise indicated the English passages of *Faust* are from the prose translation of Barker Fairley.

symbol of manifestation in time and space and the reconciliation of opposites in a dynamic process of development.[3] Some of the opposites mentioned are: individual and collective, vulgar and refined, popular and esoteric, active and reflective, temporal and eternal. The "Prelude" concludes with an indication of the scope of the coming drama.

> So on this little stage of ours you can run through the whole of creation *[den ganzen Kreis der Schöpfung]* and with fair speed make your way from heaven through the world to hell.

Like the Book of Job, *Faust* begins with a "Prologue in Heaven." The three archangels—Raphael, Gabriel and Michael—sing the praises of creation. Then a fourth, Mephistopheles, steps forward and injects his sour note.[4]

> MEPHISTOPHELES
> Since you, O Lord, are receiving once more and wish to know how we're getting on, here I am again among those present. You've never made me feel unwelcome in the past. Only you must forgive me, I can't talk big. If I tried, you'd laugh at my rhetoric. But I forget, you haven't laughed for a long time. On the sun and the planets etcetera I've nothing to report. I only see the life of man—how wretched it is. These little lords of creation haven't changed in the least. They're just as queer as they were on the first day. It would be better for them if you hadn't given them the light of heaven. They call it their reason and all they use it for is to make themselves more bestial than the beasts. With your Grace's permission, they seem to me like those long-legged grasshoppers that make their little flying jumps and then settle in the grass and sing the same old song. If only they would stay in the grass. But they bury their noses in all the dirt they find.

---

[3] See Edinger, *Ego and Archetype,* pp. 179ff.

[4] "One, two, three—but . . . where is the fourth?" (Jung, "A Psychological Approach to the Dogma of the Trinity," *Psychology and Religion,* CW 11, par. 243) Cf. Enoch 40:7. "Enoch in his vision sees the four faces of God. Three of them are engaged in praising, praying, and supplicating, but the fourth in 'fending off the Satans and forbidding them to come before the Lord of Spirits to accuse them who dwell on earth.' " (Jung, "Answer to Job," ibid., par. 673)

THE LORD
Is this all you have to say to me? Must you always come complaining? Is there never anything on earth that you approve of?

MEPHISTOPHELES
No, sir, I find it pretty bad there, as I always have. Men's lives are so miserable I'm sorry for them. Poor things, I haven't the heart to plague them myself.

THE LORD
Do you know Faust?

MEPHISTOPHELES
What? The professor?

THE LORD
He is my servant.
. . . .

MEPHISTOPHELES
What will you wager? I'll take him from you yet, if you give me permission to lead him gently my way.

THE LORD
You're free to do that for the rest of his days. Striving and straying, you can't have the one without the other.

The Lord justifies his connivance with Mephistopheles by describing the Devil as the *dynamic* factor in existence. Indeed, as the fourth part of the divine quaternity, the Devil is the Lord's dynamic aspect.

THE LORD
Man's diligence is easily exhausted,
he grows too fond of unremitting peace.
I'm therefore pleased to give him a companion
who must goad and prod and be a devil.[5]

Faust is thus a modern Job.[6] Like Job, Faust is a victim of divine connivance. Before Faust makes his wager with Mephistopheles the

---

[5] Salm translation.

[6] At the same time as Goethe was completing *Faust,* William Blake was doing his *Illustrations of the Book of Job.* See Edinger, *Encounter with the*

heavenly wager has already transpired; that is, the drama is initiated not by the ego but by the Self. This means that the guilt associated with Faust's hybris belongs not only to the ego but also to the Self. The ego's sins of pride and over-reach have purpose and meaning. The suffering they entail is shared by both ego and Self and when it is carried consciously both are transformed.

3
Nigredo

The first scene, entitled "Night," takes place in Faust's study, "a high, narrow, vaulted Gothic chamber." Faust is in a depression, the alchemical *nigredo.*[1] His prior goals and values have collapsed.

> Look at me. I've worked right through philosophy, right through medicine and jurisprudence, as they call it, and that wretched theology too.[2] Toiled and slaved at it and know no more than when I began. . . . I have no doubts or scruples to bother me, and I snap my fingers at hell and the devil. But I pay the price. I've lost all joy in life.

Life has lost its meaning and Faust is in a state of ego-Self alienation.[3] In his despair he turns to a book of magic and the unconscious is activated. He is gripped by two visionary images, first the "sign of the macrocosm."

> Oh what a unity it is, one thing moving through another, the heavenly powers ascending and descending, passing the golden vessels up and down, flying from heaven to earth on fragrant wings, making harmonious music in the universe. What a spectacle. But ah, only a spectacle.

This is a grand image of totality but only an intuitive abstraction, a product of book knowledge. Faust yearns for more substantial nourishment.

> Infinite nature, how shall I lay hold of you? How shall I feed at these

---

[1] "The *nigredo* or blackness is the initial state, either present from the beginning as a quality of the *prima materia,* the chaos or *massa confusa,* or else produced by the separation . . . of the elements." (Jung, *Psychology and Alchemy,* CW 12, par. 334. See also Edinger, *Anatomy of the Psyche,* pp. 147ff.

[2] The four traditional faculties of the medieval university.

[3] Edinger, *Ego and Archetype,* pp. 37ff.

breasts, these nurturing springs, for which I yearn, on which all life depends.

In response comes the second image, the "Earth-spirit."

How differently this sign affects me. You, Earth-spirit, are closer to me, warming me like wine and filling me with new energy. I'm ready now to adventure into life, endure the world's joy and the world's pain, wrestle with its storms, and not lose courage in the grinding shipwreck.

This inflation is quickly quashed as Faust is appalled by the Earth-spirit's full magnitude.

SPIRIT
In floods of life, in storms of action, I range up and down. I flow this way and that. I am birth and the grave, an eternal ocean, a changeful weaving, a glowing life. And thus I work at the humming loom of time, and fashion the earth, God's living garment.

FAUST
You busy spirit, roaming the wide world, how close I feel to you.

SPIRIT
You are not close. You are not equal. You are only equal to what you think I am. *disappears*

Jung interprets the Earth-spirit as Mercurius,[4] who later manifests himself as the black dog and as Mephistopheles. More immediately the "earth" principle appears as Wagner, Faust's assistant, who knocks on the door just as the Earth-spirit vanishes. This figure represents Faust as a once-born man who knows nothing about the Greater Personality. So Faust can say to him later,

You're conscious only of a single drive;
Oh, do not seek to know the other passion!
Two souls, alas, dwell in my heart,
each seeks to rule without the other.
The one with robust love's desires
clings to the world with all its might,

---

[4] See *Alchemical Studies,* CW 13, par. 105.

the other fiercely rises from the dust
to reach sublime ancestral regions.[5]

On this occasion, contact with the simple, single-souled one preserves Faust's sanity.

FAUST
To think that this prosaic voice sounded here in my room when the
air was thronged with spirits. But for once, you miserable wretch,
I'm grateful to you. You saved me from despair that was not far
from destroying me. This apparition was so tremendous, it made a
dwarf of me, a nothing.

His inflation has been pricked.[6] "I'm not like the gods. I know it
now. I'm like the worm, wriggling in the dust." A full-scale enantiodromia ensues. He contemplates death.

You hollow skull, what does your grinning say?
That brain, in the confusion of its youth,
Like mine, once sought the ethereal dawn of truth
But in the heavy dusk went piteously astray.[7]

On the one hand the skull is a *memento mori;* on the other hand,
as the rotundum, the round aspect of man, it signifies the wholeness
that lies beyond the death of the ego.[8]

Now the pendulum swings once again as Faust's eye falls upon a
bottle of poison. His inflation returns as he contemplates suicide.

What exaltation, what divine joy. And what a reversal, deserved or
not. A worm and now this. Yes, turn your back on the sweet sunlight. Tear open the gates that others shrink from approaching. The
time has come to show by your deeds that man in moral courage is
equal to the gods, bold enough to face that dark horrific cavern and

---

[5] "Before the Gate," Salm translation.

[6] *"The experience of the self is always a defeat for the ego."* (Jung, *Mysterium Coniunctionis,* CW 14, par. 778; italics in original)

[7] Luke translation.

[8] See Jung, *Mysterium Coniunctionis,* CW 14, par. 626, and "Transformation Symbolism in the Mass," *Psychology and Religion,* CW 11, pars. 363ff.

force his way to the narrow passage, girt with flames of hell, and do it serenely, even at the risk of lapsing into nothingness.

He pours the poison into a crystal goblet and raises it to his lips when he is interrupted by the sound of church bells announcing Easter. Faust declares that he lacks "the faith that fathers your miracle .... And yet, these sounds, known to me from early years, call me back to life."

> This is the song that ushered in the merry games of childhood and the festive springtime, so free, so happy. Memory, piety, holds me from this last step of all. Ring out, sweet bells. My tears come. Earth has won me back again.

The role of the Easter bells indicates that the Faust legend is an appendage of the Christian myth. As indicated earlier it is a corollary to the coming of Antichrist, a prediction embedded in the Christian scriptures. Although Easter bells rescue Faust from suicide, what he encounters on Easter day is not the resurrected Christ but rather the birth of Mephistopheles as the black dog.

On Easter Sunday Faust and Wagner go walking in the country. As they are returning Faust bursts into a paean to the setting sun.

> Mark, now, the glimmering in the leafy glades
> Of dwellings gilded by the setting sun.
> Now slants the fiery god towards the west,
> Hasting away, but seeking in his round
> New life afar; I long to join his quest,
> On tireless wings uplifted from the ground.
> Then should I see, in deathless evening light,
> The world in cradled stillness at my feet . . .
> And now at length the sun-god seems to sink,
> Yet stirs my heart with new-awakened might,
> The streams of quenchless light I long to drink,
> Before me day and, far behind, the night,
> The heavens above me, and the waves below;
> A lovely dream, but gone with set of sun.
> Ah me, the pinions by the spirit won

Bring us no flight that mortal clay can know.[9]

Faust's grandiose yearning to accompany the sun in perpetual light is immediately followed by the onslaught of darkness. He spies a black dog who soon turns out to be the prince of darkness himself.

FAUST
Do you notice the black dog running there in the stubble?

WAGNER
Oh yes. I saw it a while back. It's just a dog.

FAUST
Look again. What do you think it really is?

WAGNER
A poodle, following us the way dogs do.

FAUST
Don't you see that he's circling us and getting nearer and nearer? If I'm not mistaken, there's a streak of fire trailing behind him.

WAGNER
All I see is a black poodle. Your eyes must be deceiving you.

FAUST
I believe he's drawing magic snares round our feet and wants to come to terms with us.

WAGNER
He's just confused, because he finds we're strangers and not his master.

FAUST
The circle is narrowing, he's not far away.

WAGNER
There you see. He's no ghost, he's just a dog like any other dog, whining and lying down and wagging his tail.

FAUST
Come here. Stay with us.

---

[9] "Outside the Town-Gate," Wayne translation.

WAGNER
A silly creature. You stop, he's at your service. You speak to him, he jumps up at you. Throw something away, he'll fetch it. He'll fetch your stick out of the water.

FAUST
You must be right. It's just his tricks, no trace of a spirit.[10]

The sequence of Faust's yearning for the empyrean heights followed by his encounter with the black dog is characteristic of the enantiodromial process of the psyche. Jung writes,

> Faust's longing became his ruin. His longing for the other world brought in its train a loathing of life, so that he was on the brink of self-destruction. And his equally importunate longing for the beauties of this world plunged him into renewed ruin, doubt and wretchedness, which culminated in the tragedy of Gretchen's death. His mistake was that he made the worst of both worlds by blindly following the urge of his libido, like a man overcome by strong and violent passions. Faust's conflict is a reflection of the collective conflict at the beginning of the Christian era, but in him, curiously enough, it takes the opposite course.[11]

At the beginning of the Christian era the conflict between nature and spirit led to asceticism. Faust takes the opposite course, following certain Gnostics who claimed that one could not be redeemed from a sin that had not been committed.[12] According to Goethe, it was Faust's "striving," longing acted upon, that brought about his redemption. "He who strives and ever strives, him we can redeem."[13] Indeed, the central theme of *Faust* is "longing"—desire, love, Eros—in a word, *libido.*

Encounter with a dog is a common theme in the analytic process. A black dog signifies the alchemical chaos, descent into the uncon-

---

[10] "Outside the Town-Gate."
[11] *Symbols of Transformation,* CW 5, par. 119.
[12] The doctrine of Carpocrates. See Hans Jonas, *The Gnostic Religion,* p. 274, and Jung, "Woman in Europe," *Civilization in Transition,* CW 10, par. 271.
[13] Part II, act v.

scious. Other aspects of the dog link it with the Philosophers' Stone itself. Jung refers to the Patristic use of the dog image:

> The Gnostic parallel *Logos/canis* is reflected in the Christian one, *Christus/canis,* handed down in the formula "gentle to the elect, terrible to the reprobate," a "true pastor." St. Gregory says: "Or what others are called the watch-dogs of this flock, save the holy doctors?"[14]

In Faust's case the black dog, Mephistopheles, functions like Cerberus as an entrance to the underworld, but also serves as guide and familiar spirit, the dark aspect of the Greater Personality. It is the first, theriomorphic manifestation of Mercurius.

---

[14] *Mysterium Coniunctionis,* CW 14, par. 174n.

4
Mephistopheles

The black dog follows Faust home. In the scene "Faust's Study," he continues his lofty longings, again interrupted by the dog.

> Night has come, bringing its strange intimations and premonitions. Our better self is awakened, our unruliness, our dangerous impulses abated. Thoughts of love begin to stir in me, love of mankind, love of god . . . . Reason raises its voice again and hope revives. You long to reach the springs of life, you long for the source.
>
> Poodle, stop your whining and growling. There's no place for these animal noises beside the lofty music that I hear within me. We know that if people don't understand a thing they ridicule it, they complain about the good and the beautiful because it embarrasses them. Is the dog going to follow suit?

The dog is here equated with vulgar, collective man (the canaille), a typical shadow figure for a pedantic professor with intellectual and aesthetic pretensions. Faust tries to protect himself from the "animal noises" by turning to the New Testament.

> I must look at the original without delay and see if I can render it honestly in my beloved German. *He opens a volume and begins*
>
> The text reads: In the beginning was the word. But stop. What about this? I can't rate the word nearly as high as that. I'll have to translate it some other way. Unless I'm mistaken, the true reading is: In the beginning was the mind. But let's not be in a hurry with the first line. Can it be the mind that creates the world? Surely we ought to read: In the beginning was the energy. But no sooner do I write this than something tells me not to stop there. And now I see the light and set down confidently: In the beginning was the act. *[Im Anfang war die Tat]*

This is a key passage. Faust here reverses the direction and goal of the collective Western psyche from heaven to earth. With this revolutionary conclusion, the translation of John, the most "spiritual" of the gospels, of course could not proceed. If Faust is to opt for action he must deal with that manifestation of earthly matters, the poodle-Mephistopheles.

As if to force attention to himself the poodle now swells to alarming proportions and takes on the appearance of a threatening monster. Faust exclaims,

> But what do I see? Can it be natural? Can it be real? This poodle is swelling so. It can't be a poodle. It's more like a hippopotamus. Eyes of fire and dreadful jaws.

It is as though Faust's rewriting of the Gospel has reactivated the monster that the Gospel was designed to escape. Faust now resorts to magical signs and incantations in his struggle with the monster. Finally a transformation occurs and Mephistopheles emerges "from behind the stove, dressed like a wandering scholar."

Faust's reversal of the Christian ascetic tendency opens him up to an encounter with the untamed primordial psyche. The encounter corresponds to the theme of "struggle with the angel," the "angel" in this case being a demon from hell. The classic version of this theme is Jacob's struggle with the angel.[1] Psychologically, wrestling with an angel can be understood as an effort to deal with an activation of the unconscious by means of active imagination, thus preventing an inundation of the ego by archaic contents. Jung writes,

> [The God] appears at first in hostile form as an assailant with whom the hero has to wrestle. This is in keeping with the violence of all unconscious dynamism. In this manner the god manifests himself and in this form he must be overcome. The struggle has its parallel in Jacob's wrestling with the angel at the ford Jabbok. The onslaught of instinct then becomes an experience of divinity, provided that man does not succumb to it and follow it blindly, but defends his humanity against the animal nature of the divine power. It is "a fearful thing to fall into the hands of the living God."[2]

By Faust's efforts the black dog is transformed into Mephistoph-

---

[1] Gen. 32:24. See Edinger, *The Bible and the Psyche,* pp. 39f.

[2] *Symbols of Transformation,* CW 5, par. 524.

eles; that is, the activated unconscious content has been humanized to some extent and made available for personal dialogue. The "struggle with the angel" is not over, however. It continues throughout the entire drama, swinging back and forth between being an "onslaught of instinct" and an "experience of divinity."

In the process of active imagination, as soon as a definite figure crystallizes out of the unconscious it is advisable to ask its name. This Faust does. Mephistopheles parries the question and, in fact, never identifies himself by name. The name derives from the original Faust legend. According to the Oxford English Dictionary, the name appeared first in the German *Faustbook* of 1587 as "Mephostophiles" and is of unknown origin. However one can surmise that it may derive from Latin *mephitis,* a noxious exhalation from the earth, plus Greek *philia,* love. Mephistopheles would then mean something like "lover of the sulphurous fumes of hell."

Although he doesn't give his name, he does reply to further inquiry:

> [I am] a part of the force that always tries to do evil and always does good. . . . I am the spirit that always negates, and rightly so, since everything that comes into existence is only fit to go out of existence and it would be better if nothing ever got started. Accordingly, what you call sin, destruction, evil in short, is my proper element.

Later he reveals his full identify when he writes in the student's book, "You will be like God, knowing good and evil," and adds, "Follow the ancient text and my relation, the snake;/ Your very likeness to God will yet make you quiver and quake."[3] This is a reference to Genesis 3:5, where the serpent tempts Eve to eat the forbidden fruit.

What is the meaning of Mephistopheles, to whom Faust is about to link his fate? First of all he is the spirit of negation, Carlyle's "Everlasting No,"[4] and the principle of heroic defiance exemplified

---

[3] "Faust's Study," ii, Kaufmann translation.

[4] "Wherefore like a coward, dost thou forever pip and whimper, and go cow-

by Milton's Lucifer.[5] He is the power principle on which the very existence of the ego is based. To say no is the primal act of *separatio*, the act which establishes the ego as the arbiter of its own existence. It is the original sin that generates initial consciousness. This fact is indicated by the reference to eating the forbidden fruit whereby "You will be like God, knowing good and evil."

Thus Mephistopheles is a bringer of consciousness which involves the hard knowledge of the opposites. For Faust he also carries another meaning, the hope for life-renewal and increased intensity of experience. He exclaims:

> Books sicken me. I'll learn no more.
> Now let us slake hot passions in
> The depths of sweet and sensual sin!
> Make me your magics—I'll not care to know
> What lies behind their outward show.
> Let us plunge into the rush of things,
> Of time and all its happenings!
> And then let pleasure and distress,
> Disappointment and success,
> Succeed each other as they will;
> Man cannot act if he is standing still.
> . . . .
> Have you not heard?—I do not ask for joy.
> I take the way of turmoil's bitterest gain,
> Of love-sick hate, of quickening bought with pain.
> My heart, from learning's tyranny set free,
> Shall no more shun distress, but take its toll
> Of all the hazards of humanity,
> And nourish mortal sadness in my soul.

---

ering and trembling? Despicable biped! . . . [Then the Everlasting No pealed through my being and] there rushed like a stream of fire over my whole soul; and I shook base fear away from me forever. I was strong, of unknown strength; a spirit, almost a god. Ever from that time, the temper of my misery was changed: not Fear or whining Sorrow was it, but Indignation and grim fire-eyed Defiance." *(Sartor Resartus,* book 2, chapter 7)

[5] "Here at least/ We shall be free; th'Almighty hath not built/ Here for his envy, will not drive us hence:/ Here we may reign secure, and in my choice/ To reign is worth ambition though in Hell:/ Better to reign in Hell, than serve in Heav'n." *(Paradise Lost,* book 1)

I'll sound the heights and depths that man can know,
Their very souls shall be with mine entwined,
I'll load my bosom with their weal and woe,
And share with them the shipwreck of mankind.[6]

Or, according to another translator,

And what to all of mankind is apportioned
I mean to savor in my own self's core,
Grasp with my mind both highest and most low,
Weigh down my spirit with their weal and woe,
And thus my selfhood to their own distend,
And be, as they are, shattered in the end.[7]

The second translation brings out particularly the inflated nature of Faust's mood. Faust is striving for wholeness but as Mephistopheles tells him in the next passage, "This wholeness is only for a God." *(Dieses Ganze/ Ist nur für einen Gott gemacht!)*

Faust does not make a distinction between the ego and the Self and thus falls into a grandiose inflation which must lead inevitably to a fall. As Mephistopheles says, "Your very likeness to God will yet make you quiver and quake."[8]

Faust accepts a wager with Mephistopheles. Mephistopheles promises,

Then here below in service I'll abide,
Fulfilling tirelessly your least decree,
If when we meet upon the other side
You undertake to do the same for me.[9]

Faust agrees, providing he has an experience of total satisfaction.

If ever to the moment I shall say:
Beautiful moment, do not pass away!
Then you may forge your chains to bind me,
Then I will put my life behind me,

---

6 "Faust's Study," ii, Wayne translation.
7 "Faust's Study," ii, Arndt translation.
8 See above, note 3.
9 "Faust's Study," ii, Wayne translation.

Then let them hear my death-knell toll,
Then from your labours you'll be free,
The clock may stop, the clock-hands fall,
And time come to an end for me![10]

The wager is signed in blood. This means that Faust's commitment to Mephistopheles is not an abstract idea, but a living, affect-laden reality which has "blood" consequences. It is approximately equivalent to accepting money from a Mafia loan-shark.

What does it mean to make a pact with the Devil? From the standpoint of conventional consciousness it means having commerce with evil, the forbidden thing, the irrational, the repressed, the denied, the despicable—in a word, with the unconscious. For Christian psychology the Devil means nature, sexuality, selfishness, striving for power. Much that was represented by the pagan Great God Pan became attributes of the Christian Devil. The same can be said of Dionysus.

Faust makes his pact with Mephistopheles in his quest for personal fulfillment. He is seeking a renewal of libido, the life energy that makes existence exciting and meaningful. Beyond that he is striving for wholeness. Mephistopheles symbolizes the Greater Personality, the Self, in its dark aspect. The theme of service, who is to serve whom, is highly relevant. It points to the ultimate fact of individuation, namely, the fact that the ego is fated to serve the Self.

Goethe pictures Mephistopheles as highly intelligent, with infallible insight into the weakness and hypocrisy of humanity. He is an amoral, inhuman, observing eye similar to what Jung has called the "natural mind."[11]

The so-called natural mind . . . says the terrible things, the absolutely straight and ruthless things.[12]

Natural mind . . . is just the same as nature, the mind of trees or rocks or water or the clouds or the winds, and therefore so ruthless,

---

[10] "Faust's Study," ii, Luke translation.

[11] *Memories, Dreams, Reflections,* p. 50.

[12] Jung, *Interpretation of Visions,* vol. 5, p. 1.

so absolutely beyond man that it hardly takes man into account. . . . It has this quality of an almost animal ruthlessness along with a strange kind of superiority which reaches far beyond man. . . . Because of such superiority it is also divine.[13]

A key to the psychological understanding of *Faust* is the realization that Mephistopheles corresponds to the alchemical spirit Mercurius. Alchemy, "rather like an undercurrent to the Christianity that ruled on the surface,"[14] compensated the one-sided spiritual, light qualities of Christ, the son of the father, by producing a son—

> not the antithesis of Christ but rather his chthonic counterpart, not a divine man but a fabulous being conforming to the nature of the primordial mother. And just as the redemption of man the microcosm is the task of the "upper" son, so the "lower" son has the function of a *salvator macrocosmi*.[15]

Mephistopheles corresponds to this "lower son" who is the "son of chaos," a product of the *prima materia*, "a chthonic spirit, related to Wotan and the Devil."[16] Jung writes,

> If Mercurius is not exactly the Evil One himself, he at least contains him—that is, he is morally neutral, good and evil, or as Khunrath says: "Good with the good, evil with the evil." His nature is more exactly defined, however, if one conceives him as a *process* that begins with evil and ends with good.[17]

---

[13] Ibid., p. 5.
[14] Jung, *Psychology and Alchemy,* CW 12, par. 26.
[15] Ibid.
[16] Jung, *The Symbolic Life,* CW 18, par. 1693.
[17] *Alchemical Studies,* CW 13, par. 276.

5

Communion with Darkness

With the wager completed, Faust and Mephistopheles set off on their travels. The first stop is Auerbach's tavern where coarse drunkards are carousing. This scene and the following one are a prelude to the Faust-Gretchen love story and they present us with the ugly, infernal aspect of Eros. In the tavern a cruel song is sung.

> In a cellar nest there lives a rat,
> Had butter and lard to suit her,
> She wore a belly-bag of fat,
> A pouch like Dr. Luther.
> The cook had poison scattered out;
> That drove her hither and about
> As if she had love in her belly.
> As if she had love in her belly.
>
> She hurried, scurried, pawed and clawed,
> And swilled from every puddle,
> The house was all scratched up and gnawed,
> To soothe her frantic muddle;
> Tried many a leap in fear and pain,
> But all she tried was tried in vain,
> As if she had love in her belly.
> As if she had love in her belly.
>
> In fright she sought the light of day.
> Came running in the kitchen,
> Fell at the stove and there she lay,
> With piteous gasp and twitching.
> The poisoner only laughed, she knew
> She'd bit off more than she could chew,
> As if she had love in her belly.
> As if she had love in her belly.[1]

---

[1] Arndt translation, modified.

The repeated refrain, "As if she had love in her belly" *(Als hätte sie Lieb im Leibe),* drives home the terrible equation: love = rat poison. The alchemical texts often equate Mercurius with poison. In one text Mercurius says of himself, "I am the poison-dripping dragon. . . . From my snout there comes a spreading poison that has brought death to many."[2] "The Book of Lambspring" says,

> A savage Dragon lives in the forest,
> Most venomous he is, yet lacking nothing:
> When he sees the rays of the Sun and its bright fire,
> He scatters abroad his poison,
> And flies upward so fiercely
> That no living creature can stand before him,
> Nor is even the Basilisk equal to him.
> He who hath skill to slay him, wisely
> Hath escaped from all dangers.
> Yet all venom, and colours, are multiplied
> In the hour of his death.
> His venom becomes the great medicine.
> He quickly consumes his venom,
> For he devours his poisonous tail.
> All this is performed on his own body,
> From which flows forth glorious Balm,
> With all its miraculous virtues.
> Hereat all the Sages do loudly rejoice.[3]

Mephistopheles is the poisonous Mercurius whom Faust tries to assimilate, not without "love-pangs in the belly."[4] Similarly, Job was subjected to the poisonous onslaught of Satan. Like the poisoned rat, Gretchen is destined to die of "love in the belly." Underlying this ugly image is the psychological fact that the first stage of anima development (Eve, Nature)[5] must undergo transfor-

---

[2] Jung, *Alchemical Studies,* CW 13, par. 267, quoting the "Aurelia occulta."
[3] *The Hermetic Museum,* I, 286.
[4] Fairley translation.
[5] "Four stages of eroticism were known in the late classical period: Hawwah (Eve), Helen (of Troy), the Virgin Mary, and Sophia. The series is represented in Goethe's *Faust:* in the figures of Gretchen as the personification of a purely instinctual relationship (Eve); Helen as an anima figure; Mary as

mation through death and rebirth. The poisoned rat represents the split-off, furtive, animal aspect of the anima which cannot survive encounter with Mercurius.

As the tavern scene proceeds Mephistopheles miraculously draws wine from a wooden table as though it were a wine cask. This establishes his identity with Dionysus-Bacchus, as Heraclitus revealed long ago:

> For if it were not to Dionysus that they made a procession and sang the shameful phallic hymn, they would be acting most shamelessly. But Hades is the same as Dionysus in whose honour they go mad and rave.[6]

This symbolic equation may not seem a serious matter to the casual drinker, but for the alcoholic it is a grim reality.

The communion with darkness continues in the next scene, "Witch's Kitchen," in which Faust and Mephistopheles visit the witch with her typical witch's caldron tended by apes. Here Faust enacts an infernal Communion ritual in order to be rejuvenated.

MEPHISTOPHELES
Get me a glassful of your famous juice!
But please, the oldest you can find—
Where years of age have multiplied its strength.

WITCH
With pleasure! I keep a handy bottle on my person,
from which I snitch a little now and then.
The stink has gone from it completely.[7]

---

the personification of the 'heavenly,' i.e. Christian or religious relationship; and the 'eternal feminine' as an expression of the alchemical *Sapientia.*" (Jung, "The Psychology of the Transference," *The Practice of Psychotherapy,* CW 16, par. 361)

[6] John Burnet, *Early Greek Philosophy,* p. 141. See also Jung, *Psychology and Alchemy,* CW 12, par. 182, and *Mysterium Coniunctionis,* CW 14, par. 192.

[7] Cf. this dream: *I go out for dinner at a very special place. . . . For desert they serve "cow-dung cookies"—supposedly a delicacy like filet mignon. However they warn me to be careful, for some may not have crystallized out of their prior form. The idea of eating them causes me great distress.* (See Edinger, *Anatomy of the Psyche,* p. 111)

Yes, indeed, I'll gladly let you have a swig.
softly
But if this man should drink it when he's not prepared,
he would die within the hour, as you know.[8]

The witch's potion, like Mercurius, is poison to the unprepared.[9]

The witch recites an elaborate incantation as she prepares to administer the potion:

This you must know!
Make ten out of one,
Then let two go,
Make an even three,
Then rich you will be.
Discard the four!
Of five and six
So says the witch.
Make seven and eight,
Thus it is finished:
And nine is one
And ten is none,
This is the witch's one-times-one.[10]

The basis of this formula is the Pythagorean tetractys,[11] 1+2+3+4 = 10, also represented as a triangle:

---

[8] Salm translation.

[9] Cf. Jung's observation: *"I* call it a mistake that he [Nietzsche] ever published *Zarathustra.* That is a book which ought not to be published; it should be reserved for people who have undergone a very careful training in the psychology of the unconscious. . . . If a man reads *Zarathustra* unprepared, with all the naive presuppositions of our actual civilization, he must necessarily draw wrong conclusions . . . . Many suicides have felt themselves justified by *Zarathustra." (Nietzsche's Zarathustra,* vol. 1, pp. 475f)

[10] Raphael translation, modified.

[11] "The epitome of Pythagorean wisdom . . . . The 'tetrad' of the numbers 1, 2, 3, and 4 which add up to 10 (the 'perfect triangle'), contains within itself at the same time the harmonic ratios of fourth, fifth, and octave. The Sirens produce the music of the spheres, the whole universe is harmony and number, *arithmo de te pant' epeoiken* [everything has been made by number]. The tetractys has within it the secret of the world." (Walter Burkert, *Lore and Science in Ancient Pythagoreanism,* pp. 186f)

```
         .
      .     .
   .     .     .
.     .     .     .
```

It is a variation of the alchemical Axiom of Maria Prophetissa—"One becomes two, two becomes three, and out of the third comes the One as the fourth"[12]—which runs throughout *Faust*.

The effect of the potion on Faust is to promote anima projection. Earlier Faust had been entranced by the image of a woman of heavenly beauty in a magic mirror. Now he wants to have another look but Mephistopheles replies,

> No! No! The paragon of womankind
> Shall come before you in the flesh.
> *aside*
> With that potion in your belly
> You'll soon see Helena in every wench.[13]

---

[12] See Jung, *Psychology and Alchemy,* CW 12, par. 209.
[13] Salm translation.

6
Gretchen

The remainder of Part I is concerned chiefly with the Gretchen episode. In his desire to "slake hot passions in/ The depths of sweet and sensual sin," Faust demands that Mephistopheles arrange his seduction of the pious and innocent Gretchen.

In the scene "Evening, A Tidy Little Room," we meet Gretchen alone singing a song.

There was a king in Thule,
Was true unto the grave.
To him his dying lady
A golden goblet gave.

And he prized nothing dearer;
At feasts he drained it dry.
And when he held the goblet,
The tears would fill his eye.

And when he came to dying,
He counted land and town.
He gave all to his children,
But kept the cup his own.

With him in his great chamber
Sat knights of high degree.
They held the royal dinner
In the castle by the sea.

There stood the old carouser
And drank his last red wine:
Then flung the holy vessel
Into the foamy brine.

He saw it sway and falter
And slip into the sea;

His eyes did sink forever,
And never more drank he.[1]

Ultima Thule was an island in the northern sea regarded by the ancients as the northernmost point on the earth, on the edge of the world so to speak.[2] At the edge of human consciousness, a product of a love relationship, a golden goblet *(goldnen Becher)* or holy vessel *(heiligen Becher)* appears and is cherished for a while, only to be returned to the unconscious from where it came.

The image of the cup or goblet has come up several times before. In the first scene, "Night," Faust pours poison into a goblet of pure crystal *(kristallne reine Schale)* and prepares to drink it before being interrupted by the Easter bells. In "Auerbach's Tavern," where the rat-poison song is sung, Mephistopheles produces wine from the table to fill the glasses of the topers. In the "Witch's Kitchen" scene, Faust drinks down the bowl *(Schale)* filled with the witch's potion. In Gounod's opera *Faust,* based on Goethe, the goblet of poison and the potion of youth are the same, the one magically transformed into the other by Mephistopheles.[3]

The archetype of the bowl or vessel is one of the most basic archetypal patterns of the psyche. It signifies the experience of the feminine principle as containment and the facilitation of nourishment. According to an ancient legend the first bowl was molded on the breast of Helen of Troy. Perhaps its most exalted symbolism is found in the legend of the Holy Grail.[4] The vessel archetype is the Eternal Form or Platonic idea of the experience of containment and nourishment. It is the primordial image of the divine source that

---

[1] Salm translation.

[2] Virgil says to Augustus, "Farthest Thule owns they lordship" *(tibi serviat ultima Thule), Georgics,* vol. 1, p. 30.

[3] "And now, professor,
I invite you
to empty this goblet
wherein bubbles and smokes
not death—not anymore—nor poison
but life." (Act 1)

[4] See Emma Jung and Marie-Louise von Franz, *The Grail Legend.*

provides a containing *context* for the fulfillment of libido. As with all archetypes it is bipolar, poison or panacea, depending on circumstances.

The Grail was also considered to be a "stone,"[5] which links it with the symbolism of the alchemical Philosophers' Stone, a well-known symbol of the Self.

Basically, the vessel archetype represents the Self in its feminine aspect, or in other words, it represents the product of the coniunctio in its feminine form. The King of Thule song, with its finding and losing of the *heiligen Becher,* depicts a failed or arrested coniunctio. The song pictures symbolically the Faust-Gretchen love affair. Just as the golden goblet was tossed back into the sea so the child of the Faust-Gretchen union was not permitted to survive.

The story proceeds. Faust wins Gretchen's love and their union is consummated with the help of a sleeping potion given to Gretchen's mother. Unfortunately, the dose was too high and the mother dies. Gretchen's brother, Valentin, also dies, killed in a duel with Faust while trying to avenge his sister's dishonor. Thus Gretchen's encounter with Faust has destroyed her family containment. Her incestuous libido attachments to mother and brother have been abruptly severed.

More threatening still, her containment in *Mater Ecclesia* has been destroyed. This fact is presented with dreadful urgency in the scene titled "Cathedral." As Gretchen, pregnant and abandoned, tries to pray in church, she is assailed by the voice of an Evil Spirit telling her she is condemned to hell and beyond redemption. In the background the choir chants the ominous "Dies Irae," sequence hymn in the Burial Mass.

> *Dies irae, dies illa*
> *Solvet saeclum in favilla.*
> . . . .
> *Judex ergo cum sedebit,*
> *Quid quid latet ad parebit,*

---

[5] Ibid., pp. 142ff.

Nil inultum remanebit.

Quid sum miser tunc dicturus?
Quem patronem rogaturus,
Cum vix justus sit securus?

That day of wrath, that dreadful day
When heaven and earth shall pass away,
. . . .
The Lord of judgment on his throne
Shall every secret thing make known,
No sin escapes that once was sown.

Ah, how shall I that day endure?
What patron's aid can make secure,
When scarce the just themselves are sure.[6]

This scene parallels Gretchen's inner experience of judgment with
the Last Judgment of the world, thus equating Gretchen with the collective soul of the Christian eon. The Christian psyche is fatally split
between Christ and Satan, spirit and nature, heaven and hell. That
split is demonstrated by the image of the Last Judgment which will
separate for eternity the sinners from the saved, sending the one to
hell and the other to heaven.

Gretchen is caught in the coils of that tragic dissociation of the opposites. As she tries to realize the coniunctio, she is caught between
the dissociated opposites and must endure the suffering that is generated between that hammer and anvil.

Although Gretchen carries the major burden of suffering, Faust is
not unscathed, as is evident in the scene entitled "Dull Day, A Field,"
the only scene written in prose. Faust has just learned that Gretchen
has gone mad and is imprisoned for murdering her baby.

FAUST
An outcast, driven to despair. Wretchedly wandering the wide earth
and now at long last a prisoner, a condemned criminal, locked in a
dungeon, exposed to the cruellest torture, the dear girl and so ill-
fated. Had it come to this? . . . A prisoner. In hopeless misery. At

[6] *Mary Knoll Missal,* pp. 611f.

the mercy of evil spirits and the unsparing censure of mankind. And meanwhile you distract me with your vulgar entertainments, keep her desperate plight from me, and leave her to meet her end alone.

MEPHISTOPHELES
She's not the first.

FAUST
You beast. You foul monster . . . . Not the first! Oh the shame of it, beyond human power to comprehend, that more than one of us mortals reached this depth of misery, that the death-agony of the first was not enough to clear all the others in the eyes of the great forgiver *[ewig Verzeihenden]*. The suffering of this single one racks me, marrow and bones. But you pass over the fate of thousands with a grin, unmoved.

MEPHISTOPHELES
. . . .
Why do you have dealings with us if you can't go through with it? . . . Did we force ourselves on you or you on us?
. . . .
Who was it that brought her to ruin? Was it me or was it you?

Jung observes that although "Faust is introduced like Job . . . it is not he who suffers; it is others who suffer through him."[7] That is not totally true, as indicated by this scene. Faust exclaims that Gretchen's agony "pierces me to the marrow of my being" *(mir wühlt es Mark und Lebendurch)*. However this is not yet guilt or remorse, because Faust blames Mephistopheles and has not yet taken responsibility for his own actions.

Faust's seduction and abandonment of Gretchen has laden him with unrealized guilt. By all conventional and moral standards he should marry Gretchen. This option is not mentioned in Goethe's *Faust,* but in Marlowe's *Doctor Faustus* marriage is expressly forbidden.[8] Faust's failure to marry Gretchen can be justified only if he

---

7 *The Symbolic Life,* CW 18, par. 1694.
8 "Mephistophilis. Marriage is but a ceremonial toy,/ And if thou lovest me, think no more of it." (Act 2, scene 1)

redeems himself to society by creating a value of equal or greater worth than the value he has betrayed.

Jung writes:

> Since the breaking of [a] . . . previous personal conformity would mean the destruction of an aesthetic and moral ideal, the first step in individuation is a tragic *guilt*. The accumulation of guilt demands *expiation*. . . .
>
> Individuation cuts one off from personal conformity and hence from collectivity. That is the guilt which the individuant leaves behind him for the world, that is the guilt he must endeavor to redeem. He must offer a ransom in place of himself, that is, he must bring forth values which are an equivalent substitute for his absence in the collective personal sphere. Without this production of values, final individuation is immoral and—more than that—suicidal.[9]

Faust does not consider marriage because his goal is self-fulfillment without consideration of society. He thereby commits a crime against society for which Gretchen is punished. It is only near the end of Part II that Faust begins the service of humanity as a whole which could redeem him of his guilt.

In the final scene of Part I, Faust visits Gretchen in prison where she awaits execution. He urges her to escape with him, but, like Socrates, she refuses. She shrinks from him and calls on God.

> Lord, I am thine, oh save me and defend!
> Father, let angels now have charge of me,
> Encamped around in heavenly company.[10]

Mephistopheles announces that she is condemned but a voice from above replies, "redeemed," as Faust and Mephistopheles flee.

Understood psychologically, the Gretchen episode represents the first attempt to achieve the coniunctio. It ends in tragic failure because it happens *unconsciously*. As already mentioned, Gretchen represents the first stage in the development of the anima, the instinc-

---

[9] *The Symbolic Life,* CW 18, pars. 1094f.
[10] Wayne translation.

tual stage.[11] At this level the anima is pure desirousness. It expresses the yearning for coniunctio in an unconscious, concrete form and thus generates what I have called elsewhere the "lesser coniunctio."[12] This form of the coniunctio is followed necessarily by mortificatio, which brings frustration and suffering in the wake of the illusory delight of union. The bliss of erotic love turns into the "rat poison" of the song in Auerbach's tavern.

Gretchen is pictured as a pure, innocent and pious young woman. Indeed, her innocence was a major attraction to Faust. In terms of Faust's psychology she represents his pious Christian anima safely contained in the sacred rituals of the church. The church for her was the repository of the treasury of the archetypes and thus it was to the church that Faust's first gift of jewels was transferred. It was Faust's innocent Christian soul that was exploited and abandoned by the onslaught of Mephistophelian energy that took possession of him.

The same description applies to modern man as "the dechristianization of our world [and] the Luciferian development of science and technology"[13] reach their culmination.

---

[11] See above, p. 34, note 5.

[12] *Anatomy of the Psyche,* pp. 212ff.

[13] Jung, *Aion,* CW 9ii, par. 68.

7

Carnival

We now enter *Faust, Part II.* Part II has a strikingly different charac-
ter from Part I. Part I is personal. Part II is archetypal. In Part II it is
as though the events of Part I are repeating themselves on the level of
the collective unconscious.

To put it another way, Part I describes a conscious experience and
Part II is the accompanying dream that points to its deeper meaning.
Like a dream, Part II is confusing and ambiguous. Its images are
fluid, shifting and multifaceted in meaning; history folds in on itself;
past and present intersect; myth and reality overlap.

As Part II begins we are introduced to an emperor whose realm is
in total disarray. Lawlessness is rampant, the borders are being vio-
lated, the unpaid army is on the verge of mutiny and the government
is bankrupt. Just as Part I begins with the despair and psychological
bankruptcy of the ego represented by Faust, so Part II begins with a
similar condition on the collective or transpersonal level. This is the
familiar alchemical theme of the sick king calling for rescue or rejuvenation.[1] One example of this theme, Ripley's "Cantilena," is dis-
cussed at length by Jung.[2] Another example is the so-called "Vision
of Arisleus." A condensation of the story is as follows:

The *Rex marinus* has a kingdom under the sea, but nothing pros-
pers there and nothing is begotten because "only like mates with
like." Since there are no philosophers in the kingdom, the king calls
to the philosopher Arisleus who courageously descends to the bot-
tom of the sea for a consultation. He advises the king to mate
Gabricus with Beya, the son and daughter of the king "whom he has
hatched in his brain." However when this advice is followed a catas-

---

[1] Cf. also the ailing Fisher King of the Grail Legend and the plague-ridden
land at the beginning of Sophocles' *Oedipus Rex.*
[2] *Mysterium Coniunctionis,* CW 14, pars. 368ff.

trophe occurs. "With so much love did Beya embrace Gabricus that she absorbed him wholly into her own nature and dissolved him into atoms."

In punishment for the death of the king's son, Arisleus and his companions are imprisoned in a "triple glass house" together with the corpse of Gabricus. Here they are exposed to intense heat and "every kind of terror" for eighty days. In one version, the prison is the womb of Beya. In another, Beya asks to join the prisoners. At the end of the ordeal, Arisleus sees in a dream his master, Pythagoras, who sends him his disciple, Harforetus, "the author of nourishment." The disciple brings "the food of life" and Gabricus is revived. Pythagoras says to write down "for posterity how this most precious tree is planted, and how he that eats of its fruits shall hunger no more."[3]

This alchemical parable has several parallels with Faust's dealings with the emperor: 1) the ailing kingdom; 2) call for help from the "philosopher" (Faust-Mephistopheles); 3) descent to the depths; and 4) the coniunctio as prescription for healing. The suffering, which is part of the Arisleus vision, in *Faust* is not carried by the ego but rather by the anima (Gretchen) and even to some extent the Self.[4]

Rilke's poem *Die Konige der Welt sind alt* deals with the image of the ailing, sterile king but does not carry it to the point of regeneration.

> The sovereigns of the world are old
> and they will have no heirs at all.
> Death took their sons when they were small,
> and their pale daughters soon resigned
> to force frail crowns they could not hold.
> The mob breaks these to bits of gold
> that the world's master, shrewd and bold,
> melts in the fire to enginery
> that sullenly serves his desires,

---

[3] The quoted material is from Jung's discussion of the "Vision of Arisleus" in *Psychology and Alchemy,* CW 12, pars. 435-440, 449-450.

[4] See below, chapter 13.

but fortune is not in his hire.
The ore is homesick. It is eager
to leave the coins and turning wheels
that offer it a life so meagre.
From coffers and from factories
it would flow back into the veins
of gaping mountains whence it came,
that close upon it once again.[5]

The "sick king" theme refers to the decay of the psychic dominant and the need for the regeneration of the God-image, both in society and in the individual. Its extreme form is shown in Nietzsche's announcement that "God is dead." Occasionally in the life of the individual and the collective, the Self, the central transpersonal organizing principle, must undergo reconstitution. Only in this way can the ego reestablish its intermittently waning relation to the eternal images. Jung writes,

> Just as the decay of the conscious dominant is followed by an irruption of chaos in the individual, so also in the case of the masses (Peasant Wars, Anabaptists, French Revolution, etc.), and the furious conflict of elements in the individual psyche is reflected in the unleashing of primeval blood-thirstiness and lust for murder on a collective scale. . . . The loss of the eternal images is in truth no light matter for the man of discernment. . . . The undiscerning *(anooi)* miss nothing, and only discover afterwards in the papers (much too late) the alarming symptoms that have now become "real" in the outside world because they were not perceived before inside, in oneself, just as the presence of the eternal images was not noticed.
> . . .
> Only the living presence of the eternal images can lend the human psyche a dignity which makes it morally possible for a man to stand by his own soul, and be convinced that it is worth his while to persevere with it.[6]

Mephistopheles solves the financial problems of the bankrupt empire by a brilliant stratagem. He reminds the emperor that great

---

[5] *The Book of Hours*, II, 24, in *Poems from the Book of Hours*, p. 43.
[6] *Mysterium Coniunctionis*, CW 14, pars. 510f.

treasure lies buried in the ground.

> In mountain-veins, old walls, or underground,
> Is gold, uncoined or minted to be found.
> . . . .
> The stuff lies there: the problem is to win it;
> That calls for art, and who can now begin it?
> Yet ponder this: in times of panic flight,
> Of land and folk submerged in hostile might,
> This man or that, by urgent terror ridden,
> His dearest treasure here or there has hidden.
> 'Twas thus in mighty times of Roman fame,
> And ever more, to present day, the same.
> There, quiet beneath the ground, lies wealth untold:
> The ground's the Emperor's, and his the gold.[7]

The image of underground riches is alchemical. According to alchemical fantasy, countless revolutions of the sun have spun gold into the earth from which it can be recovered by the opus. For Mephistopheles the buried treasure derives from antiquity. In either case it represents the *values* that are associated with the eternal images hidden in the unconscious. Mephistopheles conceives a fraudulent scheme whereby he borrows on these unrealized resources by issuing paper money against them. In a succeeding scene the miracle is announced.

> We've paid off all our debts and got out of the usurer's clutches.
> . . . .
> We've issued an instalment of pay and the whole army's loyal again.
> . . . .
> Hear me then and look at this momentous piece of paper, which has turned all our woe to weal. *He reads* "To whom it may concern, this paper here is worth a thousand crowns, its collateral lying safely in the wealth of buried treasure within our borders. Steps have been taken for this treasure to be raised without delay so as to redeem the pledge."[8]

---

[7] Act 1, "Imperial Palace," Wayne translation.
[8] Act 1, "Park."

This fraudulent scheme pictures modern man's relation to both his inner and his outer values. Internally he has lost connection with the inner treasure (eternal images) and is living on psychological credit with the prospect of a final reckoning looming ever nearer. Externally he is behaving in the same irresponsible fashion. With the destruction of collective spiritual values money has taken on divine status, but even that concrete object of value is treated with reckless irresponsibility as governments resort to credit binges and deficit spending as if there were no tomorrow. The modern techniques to manipulate currency are dazzling, but as Jung reminds us, "The very objects and methods which have led civilized man out of the jungle have now attained to an autonomy which terrifies him."[9]

Modern man has lost his old God, but since nature abhors a vacuum other lesser agencies rush in to fill the void. One of these is money. For many, money is God. The notion of "economic man" vies with "sexual man" as the basic explanatory principle of human existence. Mephistopheles advises all to dig the ground for riches.

> Take spade and mattock, dig, and not by halves,
> Ply your own hands, the toil will make you great,
> And raise yourself a herd of golden calves
> That spring from earth, enriching your state.[10]

The reference is to the golden calf which enraged Yahweh against the Israelites.[11] Gounod turns the image into a brilliant sardonic aria sung by Mephistopheles.

> The Golden Calf stands mighty forever!
> Its power is enthroned
> from one end of the earth to the other.
> To honor the perverted idol
> kings and peasants alike,
> amid the murky jangle of money,
> dance in feverish whirl

---

[9] *Letters,* vol. 2, p. 608.
[10] Act 1, "Imperial Palace," Wayne translation.
[11] Ex. 32:1ff.

about the foot of this throne.
And Satan calls the tune!
And Satan calls the tune!

The Golden Calf is conqueror of gods;
in his contemptuous triumph
the servile creature ridicules heaven.
It stares down on the human race,
swarming like maniacs at its feet,
rushing pellmell, sword in hand,
wherever gleams the hope of gain!
And Satan calls the tune!
And Satan calls the tune![12]

Before the paper money scheme has been enacted, the imperial court ignores its concerns and throws itself into a pre-Lenten carnival celebration. The Emperor announces,

So let the time in merriment be passed!
Then we shall welcome the Ash Wednesday Fast.
Meanwhile we celebrate in any case
Gay Carnival at all the wilder pace.[13]

Just as Part I begins on Holy Saturday, the end of Lent, so Part II begins with Carnival, Mardi Gras, the day before the beginning of Lent. The pendulum swing between Carnival and Lent, between the libertine and the ascetic, is characteristic of the split in the Christian psyche. Carnival, meaning good-bye to meat, is an occasion to indulge briefly in greed and lust before beginning the restraint of the flesh. Preceding the Gretchen adventure, Faust immersed himself in coarse instinctuality in Auerbach's Tavern and the Witch's Kitchen. Now, preceding the Helen adventure, he again enters the realm of Dionysian excess. Jung says,

The Dionysian element has to do with emotions and affects which have found no suitable religious outlets in the predominantly

---

[12] Act. 2.
[13] Act. 1, "Imperial Palace," Arndt translation.

Apollonian cult and ethos of Christianity. The medieval carnivals and *jeux de paume* in the Church were abolished relatively early; consequently the carnival became secularized and with it divine intoxication vanished from the sacred precincts. Mourning, earnestness, severity, and well-tempered spiritual joy remained. But intoxication, that most direct and dangerous form of possession, turned away from the gods and enveloped the human world with its exuberance and pathos. The pagan religions met this danger by giving drunken ecstasy a place within their cult. Heraclitus doubtless saw what was at the back of it when he said, "But Hades is that same Dionysos in whose honour they go mad and keep the feast of the wine-vat." For this very reason orgies were granted religious license, so as to exorcise the danger that threatened from Hades. Our solution, however, has served to throw the gates of hell wide open.[14]

This Faustian Carnival does just that—it throws the gates of hell wide open. No Ash Wednesday follows this Mardi Gras.

As the Carnival progresses, we are presented with a number of classical and allegorical figures. Most striking is Plutus, the god of wealth, in a splendid carriage with four horses driven by a "Boy Charioteer." As they proceed through the crowd they scatter precious jewels, gold and coins, but it is all illusion that only frustrates the avarice it has excited. Finally, fire wells up from the underworld and threatens to consume them all. With this the Carnival ends and the masquerading figures vanish.

Plutus, the god of riches, is closely associated with *Pluton,* the Latin name for the Greek Hades, god of the underworld. They are connected symbolically because the depths of the earth are the source of precious metals.

According to Goethe, the Boy Charioteer is an earlier version of Euphorion who appears in the third act.

Euphorion is not a human, but an allegorical being. In him is personified poetry; which is bound to neither time, place nor person. The same spirit who afterwards chooses to be Euphorion appears

---

[14] *Psychology and Alchemy,* CW 12, par. 182.

here as the "Boy Charioteer," and is so far like a spectre that he can be present everywhere and at all times.[15]

Jung identifies the Boy Charioteer as the first failed effort to create the Philosophers' Stone, the first product of the coniunctio which, along with Homunculus and Euphorion, has only a fleeting existence.[16] His connection with the quaternity is indicated by the team of four horses. The Boy Charioteer very likely derives from Plato's image of the soul as charioteer who must control two horses, a good white horse and an evil black one.[17]

Plutus generates maddening avarice in the throngs as he tantalizes them by scattering illusory riches which disappear on contact. This image represents the psychology of excess—gluttony, addiction, all fulfilled desires that do not satisfy (too much money, too much food, too much alcohol, too many drugs). Behind such compulsions is the Self (Boy Charioteer) which manifests negatively and destructively when its transpersonal energies are confined to narrow, personal purposes rather than meeting a religious attitude on the part of the ego.

[15] *Conversations with Eckermann,* Dec. 20, 1829, quoted in *Goethe's Faust,* trans. Walter Arndt, p. 423.
[16] *Psychology and Alchemy,* CW 12, pars. 243, 558.
[17] *Phaedrus,* 253 d.

8

Descent to the Mothers

Like Perseus who rashly promised to bring back the Gorgon's head, Faust offers to call up the spirits of Paris and Helen for the emperor.[1] To perform this feat Faust, like Orpheus, must descend to the underworld, to the realm of "the Mothers." Mephistopheles explains:

MEPHISTOPHELES
I dislike letting out one of the higher secrets. There are goddesses throned in solitude, outside of place, outside of time. It makes me uneasy even to talk about them. They are the Mothers.

FAUST *startled*
The Mothers.

MEPHISTOPHELES
Does it give you the shivers?

FAUST
The Mothers. The Mothers. It sounds so queer.

MEPHISTOPHELES
Queer it is. Goddesses unknown to mortal men, hardly to be named by them. You'll need to dig deep to reach them. It's your fault if we have to do it.

FAUST
Show me the way.

MEPHISTOPHELES
There is no way. You'll enter the untrodden, the untreadable, the un-permitted, the impermissible. Are you ready? There'll be no locks or bolts. You'll be pushed about from one emptiness to another. Have you any notion what emptiness is? Barrenness?

. . . .

---

[1] Like the barren kingdom in the "Vision of Arisleus," the emperor's bankrupt realm needs the experience of the coniunctio for regeneration.

I see you understand the devil and I'll give you a word of approval before you go. Here, take this key.

FAUST
That little thing.

MEPHISTOPHELES
Take hold of it and don't underrate it.

FAUST
It's growing in my hand. It's shining, flashing.

MEPHISTOPHELES
Now you're beginning to see what it's worth. This key will nose out the way for you. Follow its lead. It'll conduct you to the Mothers.

FAUST *shuddering*
The Mothers. It hits me every time. What is this word that I can't bear to hear?

. . . .

MEPHISTOPHELES
Down you go, then. I might equally say: Up you go. It's all the same. Escape the created world and enter the world of forms. Take your pleasure in what has long ceased to exist. You'll see it all as drifting clouds. Swing your key and keep it from you.

FAUST *enthusiastically*
Good. I feel a new access of strength as soon as I grip it firmly. My chest expands. On to the great task.

MEPHISTOPHELES
When you come to a glowing tripod you'll know you're as far down as you can go. By the light it throws you'll see the Mothers. Some sitting, some standing or walking about. It just depends. Formation, transformation, the eternal mind eternally communing with itself, surrounded by the forms of all creation. They won't see you. They only see ghosts. You'll be in great danger and you'll need a stout heart. Go straight up to the tripod and touch it with your key.

Faust strikes a commanding attitude with the key

MEPHISTOPHELES *looking at him*

That's the way. It'll connect and follow you as your servant. Now you'll calmly ascend. Your good fortune will hoist you. And before they notice, you'll be here with it. And once you have it here you can call up hero and heroine from the shades. You'll be the first to pull it off. It'll be done and you'll have done it. The clouds of incense will turn into gods as part of the magic process and so remain.

FAUST
And what do I do now?

MEPHISTOPHELES
Let your nature will your descent. Stamp your foot and you'll go down. Stamp again and you'll come up.

Faust stamps his foot and disappears

MEPHISTOPHELES
I hope that key works. I'll be curious to know if he ever gets back.[2]

The images in this scene are central to a psychological understanding of *Faust.* Jung quotes and discusses this passage in *Symbols of Transformation,* published originally in 1912, where he says,

The *key* unlocks the mysterious forbidden door behind which some wonderful thing awaits discovery. . . .

[This refers to] the libido, which is not only creative and procreative, but possesses an intuitive faculty, a strange power to "smell the right place," almost as if it were a live creature with an independent life of its own (which is why it is so easily personified). It is purposive, like sexuality itself, a favourite object of comparison. The "realm of the Mothers" has not a few connections with the womb, with the matrix, which frequently symbolizes the creative aspect of the unconscious. This libido is a force of nature, good and bad at once, or morally neutral. Uniting himself with it, Faust succeeds in accomplishing his real life's work . . . . He needs the phallic wand in order to bring off the greatest wonder of all—the creation of Paris and Helen [the coniunctio]. The insignificant-looking tool in Faust's hand is the dark creative power of the unconscious, which reveals itself to those who follow its dictates and is indeed capable of working miracles.[3]

---

[2] Act 1, "A Dark Gallery."
[3] *Symbols of Transformation,* CW 5, pars. 180ff.

A year or two later Jung was destined to repeat Faust's descent to "the Mothers." He describes the event as follows.

In order to grasp the fantasies which were stirring in me "underground," I knew that I had to let myself plummet down into them, as it were. . . . It was during Advent of the year 1913—December 12, to be exact—that I resolved upon the decisive step. I was sitting at my desk once more, thinking over my fears. Then I let myself drop. Suddenly it was as though the ground literally gave way beneath my feet, and I plunged down into dark depths. I could not fend off a feeling of panic. But then, abruptly, at not too great a depth, I landed on my feet in a soft, sticky mass. I felt great relief, although I was apparently in complete darkness. After a while my eyes grew accustomed to the gloom, which was rather like a deep twilight. Before me was the entrance to a dark cave, in which stood a dwarf with a leathery skin, as if he were mummified. I squeezed past him through the narrow entrance and waded knee deep through icy water to the other end of the cave where, on a projecting rock, I saw a glowing red crystal. I grasped the stone, lifted it, and discovered a hollow underneath. At first I could make out nothing, but then I saw that there was running water. In it a corpse floated by, a youth with blond hair and a wound in the head. He was followed by a gigantic black scarab and then by a red, newborn sun, rising up out of the depths of the water. Dazzled by the light, I wanted to replace the stone upon the opening, but then a fluid welled out. It was blood. A thick jet of it leaped up, and I felt nauseated. It seemed to me that the blood continued to spurt for an unendurably long time. At last it ceased, and the vision came to an end.[4]

Jung's plummeting and letting himself drop corresponds to Faust's stamping his foot and disappearing. And just as Faust brought up the Paris and Helen pair, so Jung brought back the images of Elijah and Salome.[5]

Faust returns with the tripod, reminiscent of the three-legged stool, the seat of the Pythian Priestess at the Delphic Oracle.

Jung says,

---

[4] *Memories, Dreams, Reflections,* pp. 178f.

[5] Ibid., p. 181.

The underworld tripod embodies the feminine chthonic trinity (Diana, Luna, Hecate, and Phorkyads). It corresponds to the *vas hermeticum* (and the early Christian communion table of the catacombs with 3 loaves and 1 fish).[6]

It is contact with the dark realm (the infernal trinity) that gives Faust the power to evoke the images of Paris and Helen. He calls them forth; first Paris then Helen appears, and Faust responds to the epiphany.

Have I yet eyes to see? Now in my soul
Does beauty's source reveal its rich outpouring?
My fearful quest has reached a glorious goal.
How sterile was my world, my blind exploring!
This world that, since my priesthood, I behold
Desirable, deep-based, of lasting mould!
If ever I prove false, with sense grown cold,
Then may life's pulse and breath forget their duty.
That comely form enchanting once my mind,
That mirrored magic joy of womankind,
Was but a pale form-phantom of such beauty.
To you alone I vow my striving art,
My strength, affection, life with passion twined,
My worship, frenzy, love, my inmost heart.

MEPHISTOPHELES *from the prompt-box*
Be careful, or you'll overstep your part.[7]

The same scene is described by Christopher Marlowe in one of the finest passages of English literature:

Was this the face that launched a thousand ships
And burnt the topless towers of Ilium?
Sweet Helen, make me immortal with a kiss.
Her lips suck forth my soul. See where it flies!

---

[6] *The Symbolic Life,* CW 18, par. 1697. The "underworld triad" corresponds to what Jung calls elsewhere the "lower triad." See *The Archetypes of the Collective Unconscious,* CW 9i, pars. 425f, 436f, and *Aion,* CW 9ii, par. 351. The alchemical tripod is pictured in Jung, *Psychology and Alchemy,* CW 12, fig. 144.

[7] Act 1, "Baronial Hall," Wayne translation.

Come Helen, come, give me my soul again.
Here will I dwell, for heaven is in these lips
And all is dross that is not Helena.
I will be Paris, and for love of thee
Instead of Troy shall Wittenberg be sacked;
And I will combat with weak Menelaus
And wear thy colors on my plumèd crest.
Yea, I will wound Achilles in the heel
And then return to Helen for a kiss.
O, thou art fairer than the evening's air
Clad in the beauty of a thousand stars,
Brighter art thou than flaming Jupiter
When he appeared to hapless Semele,
More lovely than the monarch of the sky
In wanton Arethusa's azure arms,
And none but thou shalt be my paramour.[8]

Faust has encountered the *numinosum* and he is overwhelmed by
it. Paris and Helen represent the coniunctio that Faust wants to join.
Jung writes,

> Goethe makes the divine images of Paris and Helen float up from the
> tripod of the Mothers—on the one hand the rejuvenated pair, on the
> other the symbol of a process of inner union, which is precisely
> what Faust passionately craves for himself as the supreme inner
> atonement. This is clearly shown in the ensuing scene as also from
> the further course of the drama. As we can see from the example of
> Faust, the vision of the symbol is a pointer to the onward course of
> life, beckoning the libido towards a still distant goal—but a goal
> that henceforth will burn unquenchably within him, so that his life,
> kindled as by a flame, moves steadily towards the far-off beacon.
> This is the specific life-promoting significance of the symbol, and
> such, too, is the meaning and value of religious symbols. I am
> speaking, of course, not of symbols that are dead and stiffened by
> dogma, but of living symbols that rise up from the creative uncon-
> scious of the living man.[9]

---

[8] *Dr. Faustus,* act. 5, scene 1, lines 96-115.
[9] *Psychological Types,* CW 6, par. 202.

As Faust and those assembled in the court look on, the figures of Paris and Helen proceed to reenact the mythological abduction of Helen. "A rape," someone says, and Faust replies,

Who speaks of rape? Am I for nothing here?
Is not the key still glowing in my hand,
That led me from the solitudes so drear,
Through terror, surge, and tempest to firm land?
Here foothold is, realities abound,
Here spirit, matched with spirits, holds its ground,
And the great double spirit-realm is found.
Far though she dwelt, now is she near, divine,
Save her I will, and make her doubly mine.
Resolved! Ye Mothers, grant this, I implore!
Who knows her once must have her evermore.

ASTROLOGER
Faust, Faust, what's this you do? With mad duress
He seizes her. Now fades her loveliness.
His key towards the stripling levelled, lo,
One touch calamitous, and all is woe!

There is an explosion. Faust lies stretched upon the ground. The spirits fade away in vapour.

MEPHISTOPHELES *taking Faust upon his shoulder*
Well, there it is! With fools best have no truck,
Else may the devil himself be thunderstruck.[10]

Faust's greedy attempt to take personal possession of an archetypal figure explodes the situation and a regression follows. In Act 3 the encounter with Helen continues.

---

[10] Act 1, "Baronial Hall," Wayne translation.

9
Homunculus

Now begins the long and complex Act 2. The unconscious Faust has been transported by Mephistopheles back to his original study where he was in Scene 1. We learn that Wagner has been doing alchemical experiments trying to create a homunculus. Suddenly, with the arrival of Mephistopheles, the experiment succeeds and a living homunculus appears in the vessel. The new-born creature immediately recognizes that the arrival of Mephistopheles was the crucial factor in his production and says to him,

> What ho, the rogue! Sir Cousin, you here too?
> You're right on cue, I am obliged to you.
> A thoughtful fate has timed it well enough.[1]

Post hoc ergo propter hoc (what comes after is caused by what came before) is a sound principle when applied to the interpretation of dreams and other symbolic imagery. We can therefore say that the creation of Homunculus shortly after Faust's explosive embrace of Helen indicates a causal connection between the two. That momentary coniunctio evidently had the effect of conceiving Homunculus in the alchemical vessel. This corresponds to what sometimes happens in analysis when the ego's encounter with the unconscious has the effect of fertilizing the latter and causing a psychic conception.

Surprisingly, Homunculus addresses Mephistopheles as cousin *(Vetter)*. Earlier, Mephistopheles had announced that the snake in the Garden of Eden was a family relative *(Muhme)*. The common denominator of Mephistopheles, Homunculus and Serpent is the spirit Mercurius. They are all manifestations of the Self at different stages of development. In alchemy the homunculus (little man) appearing in the retort indicates the culmination of the opus. It is one of the forms

---

[1] Act 2, "Laboratory," Arndt translation.

of the Philosophers' Stone, that paradoxical union of the organic and inorganic realms which symbolizes the goal of the quest.

Psychologically, the homunculus signifies the birth of the conscious realization of the autonomous psyche. In dreams it may appear as a doll or statue which comes to life, representing the ego's dawning awareness of the existence of a second psychic center, the Self.

Although Homunculus has been created, Faust, the ego, remains unconscious, still suffering the effects of encounter with the archetype. Faust is dreaming and Homunculus, who can perceive his dream, describes the content.

HOMUNCULUS *astonished*
Important, this.

The bottle slips out of Wagner's hands, hovers over Faust, and shines a light on him

A beautiful setting. A clear pool shut in among trees. Women undressing. Delightful women. It's getting better all the time. But one there is outshines the rest in splendour, a woman sprung from a line of heroes, if not from the gods. She dips her foot in the transparent flood, cools her lovely body's flame in the yielding, glittering water. But what a din of swiftly flapping wings. A plunging and splashing that shatters the smooth mirror. The girls run off in fright, but she, the queen, calmly looks on and, with a woman's pride and pleasure, watches the prince of swans nestle at her knees and, gently insistent, stay. He seems to like it there. But suddenly a mist rises and quite blots out this most charming of scenes.

Faust is dreaming of Leda, Helen's mother, approached by Zeus in the shape of a swan. Upon seeing this dream Homunculus realizes that Faust must be transported to the mythological world. If he were to awaken in his dark Gothic surroundings he would die. Homunculus says to Mephistopheles,

You're only at home in the gloom. *(looking round him)* Look at this stonework, brown with age, mouldy, horrid. And pointed arches, twirligigs, so confining. If he wakes up on us, there'll be more trouble. He'll drop dead on the spot. Woodland springs, swans, naked beauties. That was his wishful dream. How could he get used to this? I, the most adaptable of men, can hardly bear it. Away with him.[2]

Faust is transported through the air to ancient Greece. As soon as he touches ground he awakens. Homunculus says,

Set our gallant friend down and life will immediately come back to him. Here in the world of fable is where he's looking for it.[3]

The "world of fable" *(Fabelreich)* is the collective unconscious. Evidently the only thing that will cure Faust of his traumatic complex caused by the encounter with Helen is an archetypal interpretation.

Keats expresses the same idea in *Endymion*.

A thing of beauty is a joy for ever:
Its loveliness increases; it will never
Pass into nothingness; but still will keep
A bower quiet for us, and a sleep
Full of sweet dreams, and health, and quiet breathing.
Therefore, on every morrow, are we wreathing
A flowery band to bind us to the earth,
Spite of despondence, of the inhuman dearth
Of noble natures, of the gloomy days,
Of all the unhealthy and o'er-darkened ways
Made for our searching: yes, in spite of all
Some shape of beauty moves away the pall
From our dark spirits. Such the sun, the moon,
Trees old, and young, sprouting a shady boon
For simple sheep; and such are daffodils
With the green world they live in; and clear rills
That for themselves a cooling covert make
'Gainst the hot season; the mid forest brake,
Rich with sprinkling of fair musk-rose blooms:
And such too is the grandeur of the dooms
We have imagined for the mighty dead;
All lovely tales that we have heard or read:
An endless fountain of immortal drink,

---

[2] Act 2, "Laboratory."
[3] Act 2, "Classical Walpurgis Night."

Pouring unto us from the heaven's brink.

Nor do we merely feel these essences
For one short hour; no, even as the trees
That whisper round a temple become soon
Dear as the temple's self, so does the moon,
The passion poesy, glories infinite,
Haunt us till they become a cheering light
Unto our souls, and bound to us so fast,
That, whether there be shine, or gloom o'er cast,
They always must be with us, or we die.[4]

In other words, once one has had a decisive encounter with the unconscious one must have an archetypal or transpersonal understanding of the psyche in order to survive.

As Faust awakens in fable land the first fable he encounters is the one he had been dreaming about, Leda and the swan.

FAUST
Now I'm awake. Oh, let them have their way with me, the incomparable forms that my eye recovers here. So marvellously am I affected. Is it dreams? Is it memories? Once before I had this joy. Cool water sliding slowly through dense and faintly swaying bushes, sliding so slowly hardly a ripple can be heard. Springs innumerable flowing together from every side to form this clear, clean, evenly shallowed bathing-pool. And healthy young women in it, the liquid mirror making the eye's delight twofold. The women playing gaily together, or boldly swimming or wading timidly, or shrieking and splashing one another. This should be enough for me to feast on, but my thought presses further. And I turn my gaze to where behind that rich green foliage the queen is concealed.

Wonderful. Swans are entering the pool from the outer bays, majestic, poised, tender, but proudly independent in the movement of head and beak. One of them seems to stand out in pride and boldness, sailing through the rest with spreading feathers, like a wave riding on waves, on its way to the queen.[5]

---

[4] *The Poems of John Keats,* p. 55.
[5] Act 2, "The Lower Peneios."

Since Helen and coniunctio with her is the central image of the work, it is fitting that Faust should first encounter Leda, Helen's mother, and the scene of Helen's conception.

Leda and the Swan is one of the ancient world's versions of the Annunciation. It is an image of the process of the incarnation of the God-image whereby the Self is born in human consciousness. According to the myth, Zeus approached Leda in the form of a swan and impregnated her. On the same night she was impregnated by her husband, Tyndareos. As a result she gave birth to two eggs.[6] From one egg came the children of Zeus (Pollux and Helen), from the other came the children of Tyndareos (Castor and Clytemnestra)—a quaternity.

Leda and the Swan was a favorite subject of many Renaissance painters who lived contemporaneously with the historical Dr. Faustus, including Leonardo, Michelangelo, Corregio and Veronese. It is psychologically significant that just as man was falling out of containment in the Christian myth, and the God-image was falling out of metaphysical heaven and into the human psyche, that just then the image of Leda's encounter with Zeus should come to the fore-ground along with other similar images such as Danäe and the Shower of Gold, Jupiter and Io, Europa and the Bull, etc. They all symbolize the human psyche's direct encounter with the *numinosum,* an encounter spared those who are safely contained in a religious faith.

One hundred years after Goethe's *Faust,* this same image is picked up by Yeats in his poem "Leda and the Swan":

> A sudden blow: the great wings beating still
> Above the staggering girl, her thighs caressed
> By the dark webs, her nape caught in his bill,
> He holds her helpless breast upon his breast.
>
> How can those terrified vague fingers push
> The feathered glory from the loosening thighs?
> And how can body, laid in that white rush,

---

[6] *Apollodorus,* iii, 10, 6-7 and note 7.

But feel the strange heart beating where it lies?

A shudder in the loins engenders there
The broken wall, the burning roof and tower
And Agamemnon dead.
                                 Being so caught up,
So mastered by the brute blood of the air,
Did she put on his knowledge with his power
Before the indifferent beak could let her drop?[7]

This image takes on crucial importance for modern man because, as Jung has put forth, the new myth concerns the continuing incarnation of deity.[8]

In his search for Helen, Faust is led to Manto the Sybil who informs him that in order to find Helen he must descend once again to the underworld. Manto invites him in.

Enter, audacious one, glad shall you be;
The gloomy way leads to Persephone.
Within Olympus' cavern foot
She lists in secret for proscribed salute.
Here did I smuggle Orpheus in of old.
Use your turn better! Quick! Be bold!

They descend [9]

While Faust visits the underworld important action goes on above. Homunculus participates in the grand Aegean Festival. This portion of *Faust* was the occasion for Jung's *Mysterium Coniunctionis*. In the foreword to that work he writes,

This book—my last—was begun more than ten years ago. I first got the idea of writing it from C. Kerényi's essay on the Aegean Festival in Goethe's *Faust*. The literary prototype of this festival is

---

[7] *The Collected Poems of W.B. Yeats,* pp. 211f.

[8] "The myth of the necessary incarnation of God . . . can then be understood as man's creative confrontation with the opposites and their synthesis in the self, the wholeness of his personality." *(Memories, Dreams, Reflections,* p. 338; see also Jung, "Answer to Job," *Psychology and Religion,* CW 11, pars. 656 ff)

[9] Act 2, "The Lower Peneios," Priest translation.

The Chymical Wedding of Christian Rosencreutz, itself a product of the traditional hieros gamos symbolism of alchemy. I felt tempted, at the time, to comment on Kerényi's essay from the standpoint of alchemy and psychology, but soon discovered that the theme was far too extensive to be dealt with in a couple of pages. Although the work was soon under way, more than ten years were to pass before I was able to collect and arrange all the material relevant to this central problem.[10]

Mysterium Coniunctionis can thus be considered an exhaustive commentary on Goethe's *Faust,* especially as it concerns its central image, the coniunctio.

The Aegean Festival, which constitutes the scene entitled "Rocky Inlets in the Aegean Sea," is too complex to summarize briefly; however, it concludes with the numinous epiphany of the sea goddess Galatea. Homunculus is overcome by love for the goddess and shatters his containing vessel against her throne.

NEREUS
What new secret is being revealed to us in the heart of the throng. What is it flames about the scallop, at Galatea's feet, pulsing alternately strong and gentle, as if with pulsations of love.

THALES
It's Homunculus with Proteus in charge. What you see is the symptoms of his imperious desire. Do I not also hear him gasping and droning in anguish? He's going to smash himself against the shining scallop-throne. There, a flame and a flash, and he's spilt himself.

SIRENS
What a luminous miracle transfigures the waves, breaking against one another in fiery sparkles. Everything is lit up, flickering, brightening. All the figures are aglow in the night. Fire is playing over the whole scene. So let Eros prevail. Eros who started everything. Hail to the sea, hail to the waves with the sacred fire over them. Hail to the fire. Hail to the water. Hail to this rare happening.

---

[10] *Mysterium Coniunctionis,* CW 14, p. xiii.

ALL
Hail to the soft breezes. Hail to the mysterious caves. Hail above all
to the four elements.[11]

Thus Homunculus follows the advice of Proteus. Thales had so-
licited his advice in these lines:

THALES
He wants advice about how to get born. The way I have it from him,
he came into the world only half-born. It's strange. He has plenty of
mental attributes, but he's very short on body. So far the bottle is
all the weight he has. He longs to be embodied properly.

PROTEUS
A real virgin birth. You're there before you ought to be.

THALES
And there's another difficulty. If I'm not mistaken, he's a herma-
phrodite.

PROTEUS
Then all the better. Wherever he lands, he'll fit in. But there's no
need to deliberate. You must make your start in the open sea. Begin
on a small scale and enjoy swallowing what is smaller. You might
grow bit by bit and rise to higher forms.[12]

And so Homunculus is carried by Proteus into the "eternal waters"
where he is "wed to the ocean," and Act 2 ends.

The drama of *Faust,* like that of the psyche, operates on several
levels simultaneously. On one level the coniunctio of Homunculus
and Galatea is the culmination of the drama; but, as Jung observes,
"both are 'stones brought to life.' "[13]

Homunculus is one expression of the alchemical Philosophers'
Stone, and Galatea in one of her manifestations was a statue that was
miraculously brought to life by the love of its creator, Pygmalion.

---

11 Act 2, "Rocky Inlets in the Aegean Sea."
12 Ibid.
13 *The Symbolic Life,* CW 18, par. 1698.

This means that the coniunctio has taken place in the transpersonal realm, the collective unconscious, the pleroma. It has not been registered by Faust, the ego, who is in the underworld at the time.

This symbolism gives us hints of the mysterious events that may take place in the depths of the psyche when the ego makes an earnest effort to come to terms *(Auseinandersetzung)* with the unconscious.

Another feature of note is that in spite of the grand, transcendent aspect of this scene, it also harks back to the ugly song in Auerbach's Tavern. Homunculus is overcome with love for Galatea. The text reads, "What you see is the symptoms of his imperious desire. Do I not hear him gasping and droning in anguish?" Like the poisoned rat in the song, Homunculus is tortured by "love pangs in the belly"; in order to put himself out of his misery he commits suicide at the throne of Galatea, which suicide is also a fertilization of the "eternal waters" by imbuing them with the essence of life.

Cosmogonic Eros and rat poison—these are the two extreme poles of the phenomenon of Love united in this coniunctio.

10

Union with Helen

In Act 3 Helen appears in full view. In majestic lines of great beauty reminiscent of Homer she is described as she returns from Troy to her husband's palace in Sparta. She enters the palace but reemerges shortly, followed by a figure of surpassing ugliness denominated as Phorkyas. In order to understand this figure we must backtrack.

In a strange interlude in Act 2 ("The Upper Penios Again"). Mephistopheles had met the Phorkyads or Graiae, three ugly crones with one eye and one tooth among them.

MEPHISTOPHELES
. . . . I'm amazed at what I see. I thought I'd seen everything, but I have to climb down and admit I never saw the like of this. They're worse than mandrakes. When you've once set eyes on this three-fold monster, no sin will ever look ugly to you again. No hell of ours, not the cruellest, would let them near its door. And here it is, rooted in beauty's land, the land proudly called antique.

Mephistopheles then takes on the shape of a Phorkyad, turning the triad into a quaternity. Now in Act 3 he appears in the form of that ultimate ugliness under the name of Phorkyas.

The unholy alliance of the Graiae with Mephistopheles can be designated the ugliness quaternity. It is one aspect of the *numinosum* in its aesthetic dimension, being the opposite pole to beauty. Symbolically ugliness and evil are closely intertwined, as are goodness and beauty (for example, *kala k'agatha*). In the coniunctio these opposites are transcended. Such a transcendence is suggested by Jung's remark that "the horrified perception of the reality of evil has led to at least as many conversions as the experience of the good,"[1] or Rilke's lines:

---

[1] *Psychology and Alchemy,* CW 12, par. 19.

> For beauty is nothing
> but the beginning of terror, which we still are just able to
> endure,
> and we are so awed because it serenely disdains
> to annihilate us. Every angel is terrifying.[2]

Phorkyas-Mephistopheles sounds this theme of the opposites as soon as he appears.

> It's an old saying, old but as true as ever, that modesty and beauty never join hands and walk the green world together. There's an old hostility between them so deep-seated that if they ever meet, no matter where, they turn their backs on one another and hurry away, modesty distressed, but beauty always bold and impudent till the day when Hades' darkness closes over her at last, unless old age has tamed her first.[3]

In her earlier appearance Helen was with Paris, whom Faust impulsively pushed aside to embrace her. This time she is with her husband, Menelaus, and Faust approaches her much more circumspectly. After first receiving her permission, by means of Mephistopheles' magic, Helen is whisked away from her husband and transported to Faust's medieval castle. Here, in contrast to his previous behavior, Faust woos Helen with profound respect, seating her on a throne and kneeling before her. The watchman Lynceus expresses the general attitude.

> Her beauty is of such command, it makes her mistress of the land. The army is abashed before her. Their hands are limp, their swords are blunted. The sun itself is cold and dull, compared with her. Beside the wonders of her face, all the rest is empty space.[4]

This time Faust is invited by Helen to join her. She says, "I want to speak with you. But come up here. Take the ruler's seat beside me and make mine secure." Now come alarms that Menelaus with a mighty army is invading the land and the chorus warns,

---

[2] "The First Elegy," *Duino Elegies.*
[3] Act 3, "In Front of the Palace."
[4] Act 3, "Courtyard of Castle."

Whoever desires to possess the fairest of women, let him be practical above all and see to his armory. Flattery may have won him earth's topmost prize, but he won't hold it easily. Cunning men will entice her away from him. Brigands will boldly carry her off. Let him give thought to this.[5]

This is a well-known sequence in analytic practice. The ego reaches to take personal possession of a transpersonal value and immediately evokes a backlash from the unconscious. The extreme version of this phenomenon is paranoia in which the ego identifies with the Self and thereby constellates the archetypal adversary (persecutor) against itself. In Faust's case he finesses the problem by handing over to his generals the task of defense and taking Helen on a honeymoon to Arcadia. This evasion will have consequences later. Faust's failure to deal with earthly reality contributed to Euphorion's defective relation to the earth.

Faust describes the idyllic land of Arcadia as follows.

Scattered cattle come cautiously to the precipice edge, but there is shelter for all in many rocky caves, where the god Pan protects them. Nature nymphs live in cool moist places in the bushy clefts, and trees crowd trees with their branch-work reaching up aspiringly to higher regions. This is the ancient forest. The mighty oaks stand stiffly, zigzagging in their contours, while the gentle maples, rich in sweet sap, rise clear and carry their weight lightly. In the quiet shade the mother-ewes' warm milk is always there for the lambs and the children. Fruit is not far to seek. Crops ripen in the fields and honey can be found dripping from a hollow trunk. This is where well-being is hereditary, cheeks and lips ever fresh and happy. Each one is immortal in his place. They are healthy. They are contented. And so in perfect days the child grows to manhood. We are amazed. We ask and ask again, whether these are men or gods. When Apollo lived among shepherds he was so like them you couldn't distinguish. Where nature rules unchallenged, all the worlds are interlocked.

Sitting down beside her

This is what we two have achieved. Let us put the past behind us.

---

[5] Ibid.

Remember you are sprung from the greatest of the gods and in a special sense belong to the early world. No fortress must enclose you.
This Arcadia lies not far from Sparta in all its eternal youth and
vigour for us to dwell in with delight. If you agreed to live on such a
heavenly soil you would reach the happiest consummation. Our
thrones would turn into arbours. Let us accept this Arcadian joy and
freedom.[6]

Arcadia as a literary theme is

a pastoral paradise ruled by Pan, the god of flocks and herds, and in-
habited by shepherds and shepherdesses, and nymphs and Satyrs, who
dwell in an atmosphere of romantic love. . . . The idealized rural retreat, the place of escape from the reality and complexity of life in
town and court, is fundamental to the idea of Arcadia.[7]

Psychologically Arcadia corresponds, on the personal level, to the
nostalgic longing for carefree childhood. On the archetypal level it is
symbolically equivalent to the Garden of Eden or the first Golden
Age of humanity, representing original wholeness, the divinity out of
which the ego is born and the source of regeneration.

Faust's regeneration in Arcadia is symbolized by Euphorion who
is born from the union of Helen and Faust. The divine child was

wonderful. . . . Round his head there was a halo. Where it came
from, hard to say. Was it gold he was wearing? Was it mental energy
flaming? Announcing, as he stood there in his boyhood, he was
master-to-be of the beautiful, one through whose limbs the eternal
melodies sounded.[8]

Euphorion is filled with a wild desire to overcome all earthly
shackles. He climbs a tall cliff seeking a larger and larger view until
finally he tries to fly and plunges to his death. He calls for his mother
to join him and Helen vanishes from Faust's sight.

Once again the product of the coniunctio has been destroyed.
Faust's heroic effort to commandeer an archetype has failed. Jung
writes,

---

6 Ibid.

7 James Hall, *Dictionary of Subjects and Symbols in Art*, pp. 30f.

8 Act 3, "Rocky Caves."

The essential Faustian drama is expressed most graphically in the scene between Paris and Helen. To the medieval alchemist this episode would have represented the mysterious *coniunctio* of Sol and Luna in the retort; but modern man, disguised in the figure of Faust, recognizes the projection and, putting himself in the place of Paris or Sol, takes possession of Helen or Luna, his own inner, feminine counterpart. The objective process of the union thus becomes the subjective experience of the artifex; instead of watching the drama, he has become one of the actors. Faust's personal intervention has the disadvantage that the real goal of the entire process—the production of the incorruptible substance—is missed. Instead Euphorion, who is supposed to be the *filius philosophorum,* imperishable and "incombustible," goes up in flames and disappears—a calamity for the alchemist and an occasion for the psychologist to criticize Faust, although the phenomenon is by no means uncommon. For every archetype, at its first appearance and so long as it remains unconscious, takes possession of the whole man and impels him to play a corresponding role. Consequently Faust cannot resist supplanting Paris in Helen's affections, and the other "births" and rejuvenations, such as the Boy Charioteer and the Homunculus, are destroyed by the same greed. This is probably the deeper reason why Faust's final rejuvenation takes place only in the post-mortal state, i.e., is projected into the future. Is it a mere coincidence that the perfected figure of Faust bears the name . . . of one of the most famous of the early alchemists: "Marianus" or, in its more usual spelling, Morienus?

By identifying with Paris, Faust brings the *coniunctio* back from its projected state into the sphere of personal psychological experience and thus into consciousness. This crucial step means nothing less than the solution of the alchemical riddle, and at the same time the redemption of a previously unconscious part of the personality. But every increase in consciousness harbours the danger of inflation, as is shown very clearly in Faust's superhuman powers.[9]

Thus, Faust's rash action to claim Helen as his own is paradoxically *both* a sinful inflation *and* a necessary deed of heroic enterprise. This pictures the hybris of the modern ego which brings archetypal energies into the range of human consciousness but at the price of dangerous inflation.

---

[9] *Psychology and Alchemy,* CW 12, pars. 558f.

It is a psychological rule that when an archetype has lost its meta-physical hypostasis, it becomes identified with the conscious mind of the individual, which it influences and refashions in its own form. And since an archetype always possesses a certain numinosity, the integration of the numen generally produces an inflation of the sub-ject. It is therefore entirely in accord with psychological expectations that Goethe should dub his Faust a Superman. In recent times this type has extended beyond Nietzsche into the field of political psy-chology, and its incarnation in man has had all the consequences that might have been expected to follow from such a misappropriation of power.[10]

---

[10] Jung, *Psychology and Religion*, CW 11, par. 472.

11
War

The beginning of Act 4 finds Faust on a high mountain peak. In a clear reference to Christ's temptation by Satan,[1] Mephistopheles inquires,

> Is there nothing that satisfies you on this earth of ours? You're so hard to please. You've surveyed the kingdoms of the world and the glory of them in all their vastness. Is there anything at all you'd like to do?

Faust takes the bait and replies, there is, indeed, "One great thing did tempt me."[2] He proceeds,

FAUST
The open sea arrested my attention. I watched it and saw how it mounted and mounted and then relaxed and spilt its storm-waves along the level shore. And this annoyed me. A man of free mind, who respects the rights of others, is always uneasy when he sees arrogance asserting itself immoderately, violently. And it was like this here. I thought it might be an accident and I looked again more closely. The waves halted, rolled back, and withdrew from their proud conquest. The hour will come and they'll do it all over again.

MEPHISTOPHELES *to the audience*
Nothing new in that for me. I've seen it for hundreds and thousands of years.

FAUST *excitedly*
The water comes creeping up, barren in itself, to spread its barrenness wherever it goes, in every hole and corner. Now it has flooded

---

[1] "Again, the devil taketh him up into an exceeding high mountain, and sheweth him all the kingdoms of the world, and the glory of them; and saith unto him, All these things will I give thee, if thou wilt fall down and worship me." (Matt, 4:8,9)
[2] Act 4, "High Mountain," Arndt translation.

that desolate stretch of land and there waves upon waves run riot. Then they recede and nothing has been gained. It nearly drives me mad to see the elements so uncontrolled, wasting their energy so blindly. And here my spirit goes all out and boldly resolves to make this its battleground and prove itself the master.

And it is possible. With its fluid nature water can slip past any hillock. However much it rages, a slight rise can divert it, a slight drop can pull it down. Seeing this, I quickly made my plans: Get permission to exclude the imperious ocean from the shore, set limits to its watery expanse and force it back on itself. What satisfaction that would be! Step by step I thought it out. This is my wish. Help me to achieve it.[3]

Jung notes that after each erotic episode, "there follows the suppression of Eros by the power drive."[4] After the seduction of Gretchen comes Walpurgisnacht which "equals overpowering by the shadow."[5] Now after the death of Euphorion and the disappearance of Helen, "once again the next and last phase begins with the power drive."[6] It is the same temptation to power that Christ was exposed to. Jung writes,

The story of the Temptation clearly reveals the nature of the psychic power with which Jesus came into collision: it was the power-intoxicated devil of the prevailing Caesarean psychology that led him into dire temptation in the wilderness. This devil was the objective psyche that held all the peoples of the Roman Empire under its sway, and that is why it promised Jesus all the kingdoms of the earth, as if it were trying to make a Caesar of him. Obeying the inner call of his vocation, Jesus voluntarily exposed himself to the assaults of the imperialistic madness that filled everyone, conqueror and conquered alike. In this way he recognized the nature of the objective psyche which had plunged the whole world into misery and had begotten a yearning for salvation that found expression even in the pagan poets. Far from suppressing or allowing himself to be suppressed by this psychic onslaught, he let it act on him consciously, and assimilated

---

[3] Act 4, "High Mountain."
[4] *The Symbolic Life,* CW 18, par. 1696.
[5] Ibid.
[6] Ibid., par. 1699.

it. Thus was world-conquering Caesarism transformed into spiritual kingship, and the Roman Empire into the universal kingdom of God that was not of this world.[7]

Now, at the end of the Christian eon, that pattern is repeating itself with Faustian man. He is confronted with the conflict between love and power and must find a reconciling symbol which can unite these opposites. According to Jung this is how Christ resolved the problem of the Temptation.

> We say that the devil tempted him (Christ), but we could just as well say that an unconscious desire for power confronted him in the form of the devil. Both sides appear here: the light side and the dark. The devil wants to tempt Jesus to proclaim himself master of the world. Jesus wants not to succumb to the temptation; then, thanks to the function that results from every conflict, a symbol appears: it is the idea of the Kingdom of Heaven, a spiritual kingdom rather than a material one. Two things are united in this symbol, the spiritual attitude of Christ and the devilish desire for power. Thus the encounter of Christ with the devil is a classic example of the transcendent function. It appears here in the form of an involuntary personal experience. But it can be used as a method too; that is, when the contrary will of the unconscious is sought for and recognized in dreams and other unconscious products. In this way the conscious personality is brought face to face with the counter-position of the unconscious. The resulting conflict—thanks precisely to the transcendent function—leads to a symbol uniting the opposed positions. The symbol cannot be consciously chosen or constructed; it is a sort of intuition or revelation. Hence the transcendent function is only usable in part as a method, the other part always remains an involuntary experience.[8]

Faust, at first, finds no reconciling symbol. He identifies with the power image.

> It nearly drives me mad to see the elements so uncontrolled, wasting their energy so blindly. And here my spirit goes all out and boldly resolves to make this its battleground and prove itself the master.

---

[7] *The Development of Personality,* CW 17, par. 309.

[8] *Letters,* vol. 1, pp. 267f.

This is the power principle speaking. Only later, at the moment of Faust's death, do we get a glimpse of the reconciling symbol that resolves the conflict.[9]

For now, Faust is committed to war and it is psychologically fitting that no sooner does Faust proclaim his battle to be the master of the elements than the text reports "distant drums and martial music," and we learn that the emperor is at war with a rival emperor.

War is an integral feature of the Paris-Helen myth. By taking Paris' place Faust has entered that myth and must live it out.[10] Like Paris, Faust's involvement with Helen brings on war. We have already noted that in Act 3 the transporting of Helen to Faust's castle was followed by the appearance of Menelaus' army. Faust evaded the conflict then, but now it is upon him.

War (conflict at all levels) is a basic feature of coniunctio symbolism. It signifies the activated conflict between the opposites which is an inevitable prelude to their union.[11] Heraclitus says, "War is the father of all and king of all."[12] To embrace Helen of Troy means war for the same reason that Ares is the lover of Aphrodite. Love and power are the fundamental motivations of existence and are in perpetual war within the psyche, always calling for a reconciling third. (Freud, Adler, Jung!)

Literal war is an exteriorization (projection) of the coniunctio drama going on in the collective psyche. Since individuation can be achieved only by individuals (even though individuation symbolism appears in collective phenomena) that means that the conflict of opposites must be returned to the individual psyche. Only there can the reconciling symbol emerge.

> If the projected conflict is to be healed, it must return into the psyche of the individual, where it had its unconscious beginnings. He

---

9 See below, chapter 13.

10 See below, the appendix, for a psychological discussion of this myth.

11 Jung begins *Mysterium Coniunctionis* with this sentence: "The factors which come together in the coniunctio are conceived as opposites, either confronting one another in enmity or attracting one another in love."

12 G.S. Kirk and J.E. Raven, *The Presocratic Philosophers*, p. 195.

must celebrate a Last Supper with himself, and eat his own flesh and drink his own blood; which means that he must recognize and accept the other in himself. But if he persists in his one-sidedness, the two lions [opposites] will tear each other to pieces. Is this perhaps the meaning of Christ's teaching, that each must bear his own cross? For if you have to endure yourself, how will you be able to rend others also?[13]

The rest of Act 4 is concerned with the war between the rival emperors. With the help of Mephistopheles' magic, the original emperor is victorious and, in gratitude, he leases the shoreline of the realm to Faust for his project of reclaiming land from the sea.

---

[13] Jung, *Mysterium Coniunctionis,* CW 14, par. 512.

12

Baucis and Philemon

Part I of *Faust* consists of one act in many scenes. Part II is divided into five acts. On close examination it seems that the symbolism of the four elements may be behind this division. Act 1 has *fire* as a predominant content. For Act 2 the element is *water.* For Act 3 it is *air* with Euphorion's effort to fly. Act 4 involves a coming down to *earth* as Faust confronts the reality of conflict. By this reasoning the fifth and final act will be the *quintessence* in which the differentiated four elements unite in a "fifth essence" which is their unity.

In Act 5 Faust is preoccupied with a project of reclaiming land that has been under water. Greedy in his success, he is determined to own all the land in the region. However, Baucis and Philemon who live in the area refuse to sell their little cottage. Faust assigns to Mephistopheles the task of removing them forcibly. Although it was not intended, the job was botched and the elderly pair were killed. Mephistopheles reports to Faust.

MEPHISTOPHELES AND THE THREE.[1]
Here we return in full career;
It was not smoothly done, I fear.
We knocked, we rapped, we knocked in vain,
No one would open up; again
We knocked and rattled somewhat more,
And inward fell the brittle door.
We called and threatened more than once,
And still we met with no response.
As at such times it will occur,
They wouldn't hear, so didn't stir.
So we fell to without ado
And nimbly moved them out for you.
The couple did not suffer much,

---

[1] See below.

From fear fell lifeless at our touch.
A lurking stranger who was found
And offered fight, was laid aground.
Live embers, knocked about a bit
In brief but furious struggling, lit
Some straw—and now it blazes free,
A funeral pyre for those three.

FAUST
So you have turned deaf ears to me!
I meant exchange, not robbery.
This thoughtless violent affair,
My curse on it, for you to share!

CHORUS
That ancient truth we will recite:
Give way to force, for might is right;
And would you boldly offer strife,
Then risk your house, estate, and—life.[2]
[Exeunt]

In dealing with Baucis and Philemon, Mephistopheles had the assistance of three giants (3 + 1). Now another quaternity visits Faust. At midnight "four grey women" appear and try to enter Faust's house. They are named Lack *(Mangel)*, Debt-Guilt *(Schuld)*, Care *(Sorge)* and Need *(Not)*. Three of them announce, "The door is locked. We can't get in and we don't wish to. A rich man lives here." The fourth one, Care, slips through the keyhole and enters the house as her three sisters leave (again, 3 + 1). In this sequence there is a striking juxtaposition of two quaternities, indicating that the Self is constellated and is motivating the occurrence of events.

As a rich man, Faust is not subject to lack, need or debt. However, the German word for debt *(Schuld)* also means guilt.[3] This linguistic ambiguity is not incidental. It goes to the heart of Faust's defect. Although he wreaks havoc on those around him, he seems in-

---

[2] Act 5, "Deep Night," Arndt translation.

[3] According to the Lutheran Bible (Matt. 26:66), the high priests condemned Jesus saying, *"Er ist des todes schuldig."* (He is guilty of death.)

capable of true guilt or remorse. Guilt does not gain entry to his soul. However Care has now entered and she confronts him as a representative of the four. Faust refuses to acknowledge Care just as he has refused to experience guilt. Care leaves with a parting curse. She breathes on Faust and blinds him.

For the psychologist, Faust's spurning of Care is an ominous event. It means that Faust maintains his heroic stance to the end and thus remains split within himself. The Care anima, if accepted, could bring recognition of his feelings of guilt and remorse and thus lead to healing of his dissociation and redemption in this life rather than in the life beyond.[4]

Faust's failure to acknowledge Care means that he must go to his death laden with unconscious guilt. Just as Part I ends with the guilt-laden abandonment of Gretchen, so Part II concludes with the guilt-producing deaths of Baucis and Philemon.

> In his blind urge for superhuman power, Faust brought about the murder of Philemon and Baucis. Who are these two humble old people? When the world had become godless and no longer offered a hospitable retreat to the divine strangers Jupiter and Mercury, it was Philemon and Baucis who received the superhuman guests. And when Baucis was about to sacrifice her last goose for them, the metamorphosis came to pass: the gods made themselves known, the humble cottage was changed into a temple, and the old couple became immortal servitors at the shrine.[5]

Faust represents modern man, who, in his hybris, has destroyed the living connection with the gods (the *numinosum*) and has incurred a heavy load of guilt. This matter was profoundly troubling to Jung.

> All of a sudden and with terror it became clear to me that I have taken over *Faust as my heritage,* and moreover as the advocate and avenger of Philemon and Baucis, who, unlike Faust the superman,

---

[4] H.-J. Wilke discusses this matter in *"Faust und die Sorge Anmerkungen zur Ueberwindung des Heroischen"* (Faust and Care Notes on the Overcoming of the Heroic), *Analytische Psychologie,* vol. 20, no. 1 (1989), pp. 4-18.

[5] Jung, *Psychology and Alchemy,* CW 12, par. 561.

are the hosts of the gods in a ruthless and godforsaken age.[6]

And in *Memories, Dreams, Reflections,* Jung says,

I consciously linked my work to what Faust had passed over: respect for the eternal rights of man, recognition of "the ancient," and the continuity of culture and intellectual history.[7]

In addition, he took upon himself the guilt that Faust evaded. Over the entrance to his country retreat at Bollingen, he carved the inscription: *Philemonis Sacrum—Fausti Poenitentia* (Shrine of Philemon— Repentance of Faust).[8]

---

[6] *Letters,* vol. 1 (Jan. 5, 1942), pp. 309f.

[7] *Memories, Dreams, Reflections,* p. 235.

[8] See above, p. 12, and Aniela Jaffé, *C.G. Jung: Word and Image,* pp. 188f.

13
Redemption

We come now to Faust's final speech which is deeply ambiguous. He is blind. Hearing sounds of digging he assumes that ditches are being dug to drain a final marsh. Actually his grave is being dug. Out of this illusion grows a final grand fantasy.

FAUST
There is a swamp, skirting the base of the hills, a foul and filthy blot on all our work. If we could drain and cleanse this pestilence, it would crown everything we have achieved, opening up living space for many millions. Not safe from every hazard, but safe enough. Green fields and fruitful too for man and beast, both quickly domiciled on new-made land, all snug and settled under the mighty dune that many hands have built with fearful toil. Inside it life will be a paradise. Let the floods rage and mount to the dune's brink. No sooner will they nibble at it, threaten it, than all as one man run to stop the gap. Now I am wholly of this philosophy. This is the farthest human wisdom goes: The man who earns his freedom every day, alone deserves it, and no other does. And, in this sense, with dangers at our door, we all, young folk and old, shall live our lives. Oh how I'd love to see that lusty throng and stand on a free soil with a free people. Now I could almost say to the passing moment: Stay, oh stay a while, you are beautiful. The mark of my endeavors will not fade. No, not in ages, not in any time. Dreaming of this incomparable happiness, I now taste and enjoy the supreme moment.[1]

This passage corresponds to modern man's fantasy of "progress" and "perfectibility." It is based on blindness. What seems progress to Faust is actually his grave. This perhaps alludes to the collective catastrophe in store for Western man.[2] Nevertheless, the final lines

---

[1] Act 5, "Great Courtyard of the Palace."
[2] "Today we are confronted with a crisis of Western civilization whose outcome appears to be exceedingly dubious." (Jung, *Aion,* CW 9ii, par. 150)

express a profound insight that is probably responsible for Faust's redemption.

> Oh such a throng I long to see
> Treading free ground with people that are free!
> Then could I bid the passing moment:
> 'Linger a while, thou art so fair!'
> The traces of my earthy days can never
> Sink in the aeons unaware.
> And I, who feel ahead such heights of bliss,
> At last enjoy my highest moment—this.[3]

With these words Faust dies.

Now at last emerges the reconciling symbol spoken of earlier,[4] which unites the opposites love and power. Love of humanity and war against the primordial unconscious are united in the image, "Oh such a throng I long to see/ Treading free ground with people that are free!" This is an image of the creation of *consciousness,* a product of the coniunctio of love and power: confrontation with the primordial psyche united with love of humanity, something akin to Nietzsche's *amor fati.*

In this passage Faust is anticipating his highest moment in "fore-feeling" *(Vorgefühl),* not yet experiencing it concretely. By this trick he wriggles out of his wager with Mephistopheles. However, on a deeper level, he is saved because he has succeeded in creating the Philosophers' Stone. This is revealed in the words, "The traces of my earthly days can never/ Sink in the aeons unaware." *(Es kann die Spur von meinen Erdetagen/ Nicht in Aönen untergehn.)* Literally, what cannot disappear in the course of the aeons is the "track" *(Spur)* of his earthly days, that is, the indelible footprints he has left in the sands of time. This is a reference to the "incorruptible body," the permanent deposit that the individuated ego leaves in the objective psyche.[5]

---

[3] Act 5, "Forecourt of the Palace," MacNiece translation, modified.

[4] See above, pp. 78-79.

[5] See Edinger, *The Creation of Consciousness,* pp. 25ff, and *Ego and Archetype,* pp. 218ff.

During his near-death experience Jung became aware of an inde-structible life-residue. As he was about to enter the gateway to the beyond, he says, "A strange thing happened":

I had the feeling that everything was being sloughed away; every-thing I aimed at or wished for or thought, the whole phantasmagoria of earthly existence, fell away or was stripped from me—an ex-tremely painful process. Nevertheless, something remained; it was as if I now carried along with me everything I had ever experienced or done, everything that had happened around me. I might also say: it was with me, and I was it. I consisted of all that, so to speak. I con-sisted of my own history, and I felt with great certainty: this is what I am. "I am this bundle of what has been, and what has been accom-plished."

This experience gave me a feeling of extreme poverty, but at the same time of great fullness. There was no longer anything I wanted or desired. I existed in an objective form; I was what I had been and lived. At first the sense of annihilation predominated, of having been stripped or pillaged; but suddenly that became of no consequence. Everything seemed to be past; what remained was a *fait accompli,* without any reference back to what had been. There was no longer any regret that something had dropped away or been taken away. On the contrary: I had everything that I was, and that was everything.[6]

This "bundle of what has been, and what has been accomplished" corresponds to Faust's "traces of my earthly days."

Calling in devils from hell to help him, Mephistopheles hovers around the grave of Faust waiting to catch his soul as it leaves the body. However a host of angels descends from heaven scattering roses which disperse the devils and ignite in Mephistopheles tortur-ing flames of erotic desire.

MEPHISTOPHELES
My head's on fire, my heart, my liver too. This is a more devilish element. It's much crueller than hell-fire. So this is why unhappy lovers, when rejected, crane their necks in search of the one they wanted.
. . . .

---

[6] *Memories, Dreams, Reflections,* pp. 290f.

Is this the element of love? My whole body's on fire . . .
. . . .
I'm just like Job, my whole body a mass of sores, making me shudder at sight of myself.[7]

While Mephistopheles is distracted by his lust for the angels they carry off Faust's "immortal part" *(Unsterbliches).*

This is an interesting twist to the Job story. Instead of Faust's experiencing Job's suffering it falls to Mephistopheles. Psychologically this means that suffering has shifted from the ego to the objective psyche. Mephistopheles, as the spirit Mercurius, is being humanized and thereby "fixed" to the conditions of earthly mortality.[8] This is evidently a consequence of Faust's insight regarding his immortal part. It is analogous to Jung's observation that Job's insight into the nature of Yahweh requires Yahweh to become man.[9] With a relative increase in consciousness a "transfer of substance" takes place between ego and Self: the ego is eternalized and the Self is humanized.

As the angels are claiming Faust's immortal part they sing,

On to the Light
Loving flames speed!
Those damned by deeds,
May the Truth heal;
That they from evil
Be gladly delivered,
And in the totality
Blessed will be.[10]

The use of the term totality *(Allverein)* again indicates that Faust achieved a measure of individuation. This is also indicated by the pair of heavenly quaternities in the final scene. One quaternity con-

---

[7] Act 5, "Gloria."

[8] Cf. alchemical pictures of the Mercurial serpent transfixed to a tree or a cross; e.g., Jung, *Psychology and Alchemy,* CW 12, figs. 150, 217.

[9] "Yahweh must become man precisely because he has done man a wrong. . . . Because his creature has surpassed him he must regenerate himself." ("Answer to Job," *Psychology and Religion,* CW 11, par. 640)

[10] Act 5, "Gloria," author's translation.

sists of Pater Ecstaticus, Pater Profundus, Pater Seraphicus plus Doctor Marianus (3 + 1).[11] The other quaternity consists of Magna Peccatrix,[12] the Samaritan woman,[13] Mary of Egypt[14] plus Gretchen (3 + 1).

In each case the triad of figures deriving from traditional ecclesiastical iconography is completed by a personal or historical figure. Dr. Marianus probably alludes to "an eighth-century alchemist, Morienes, Morienus, Marianus, who was one of the most spiritual of all alchemists and understood the *opus* as a human transformation system."[15] In the other case it is the repentant redeemed Gretchen who completes the quaternity, emphasizing the crucial aspect of the *human* dimension in the process.[16]

Faust is now ushered into heaven under the guidance of Gretchen and the play ends with these famous lines:

Alles Vergangliche	All things transitory
Ist mir ein Gleichnis;	Are only symbols;
Das Unzulängliche	The insufficient
Hier wirds Ereignis;	Here finds fulfillment;
Das Unbeschreibliche	The indescribable
Hier ist es getan	Here it is done
Das Ewig-Weibliche	The Eternal-Womanly
Zieht uns hinan.	Draws us above.[17]

---

[11] The three Paters "indicate a hierarchy of ascending degrees of divine knowledge." *(Faust,* Arndt translation, p. 301n)

[12] "And, behold, a woman in the city, which was a sinner, when she knew that Jesus sat at meat in the Pharasee's house, brought an alabaster box of ointment." (Luke 7:37)

[13] John 4:7ff.

[14] A prostitute who felt an invisible hand preventing her from entering the church in Jerusalem. She did penance in the desert. See *The Golden Legend,* pp. 228ff.

[15] Jung, *The Symbolic Life,* CW 18, par. 1699.

[16] "[Goethe's] glorification of the Mother who is great enough to include in herself both the Queen of Heaven and Maria Aegyptiaca is supreme wisdom and profoundly significant for anyone willing to reflect upon it." (Jung, "Psychological Aspects of the Mother Archetype," *The Archetypes and the Collective Unconscious,* CW 9i, par. 190)

[17] Author's translation.

Understood psychologically, the conclusion of *Faust* is ambiguous. Although, as already noted, there is definite evidence of individuation achieved, nevertheless, the full coniunctio of the opposites has not taken place. The Christian split between heaven and hell persists and Mephistopheles has not been clearly incorporated into the divine totality. This ambiguity is due to the fact that Goethe stood right on the borderline between Judeo-Christian man and Jungian man. He was a harbinger of things to come but did not realize fully in his own being what he was writing about. Jung considers the conclusion of *Faust* unsatisfactory.

[Faust's] death, although necessary in his day and generation, is hardly a satisfactory answer. The rebirth and transformation that follow the *coniunctio* take place in the hereafter, i.e., in the unconscious—which leaves the problem hanging in the air. We all know that Nietzsche took it up again in *Zarathustra*, as the transformation into the superman; but he brought the superman into dangerously close proximity with the man-in-the-street. By so doing he inevitably called up all the latter's reserves of anti-Christian resentment, for his superman is the overweening pride, the hybris, of individual consciousness, which must necessarily collide with the collective power of Christianity and lead to the catastrophic destruction of the individual. We know just how, and in what an exceedingly characteristic form, this fate overtook Nietzsche, *tam ethice quam physice*. And what kind of an answer did the next generation give to the individualism of Nietzsche's superman? It answered with a collectivism, a mass organization, a herding together of the mob, *tam ethice quam physice,* that made everything that went before look like a bad joke. Suffocation of the personality and an impotent Christianity that may well have received its death-wound—such is the unadorned balance sheet of our time.

Faust's sin was that he identified with the thing to be transformed and that had been transformed. Nietzsche overreached himself by identifying his ego with the superman Zarathustra, the part of the personality that was struggling into consciousness. But can we speak of Zarathustra as a part of the personality? Was he not rather something superhuman—something which man is not, though he has his share in it? Is God really dead, because Nietzsche declared that he had not been heard of for a long time? May he not have come back in the guise of the superman?

. . . .

An inflated consciousness is always egocentric and conscious of nothing but its own existence. It is incapable of learning from the past, incapable of understanding contemporary events, and incapable of drawing right conclusions about the future. It is hypnotized by itself and therefore cannot be argued with. It inevitably dooms itself to calamities that must strike it dead.

. . . .

What we may learn from the models of the past is above all this: that the psyche harbours contents, or is exposed to influences, the assimilation of which is attended by the greatest dangers. If the old alchemists ascribed their secret to matter, and if neither Faust nor Zarathustra is a very encouraging example of what happens when we embody this secret in ourselves, then the only course left to us is to repudiate the arrogant claim of the conscious mind to be the whole of the psyche, and to admit that the psyche is a reality which we cannot grasp with our present means of understanding.[18]

The traditional legends end with Faust's being dragged into hell (like his cousin Don Juan). Goethe's *Faust* ends with his elevation to heaven. With more complete individuation the split between heaven and hell is healed and a third position achieved beyond the antithesis of damnation and salvation.

---

[18] *Psychology and Alchemy,* CW 12, pars. 559ff.

14
Epilogue

> What makes Goethe's *Faust* so profoundly significant is that it
> formulates a problem that had been brewing for centuries, just as
> *Oedipus* did for the Greek sphere of culture: how to extricate our-
> selves from between the Scylla of world-renunciation and the
> Charybdis of its acceptance.
> —Jung, *Symbols of Transformation.*

The basic themes that run throughout *Faust* are:
1) Descent to the underworld *(Nekyia);*
2) Love in all its aspects (libido);
3) The opposites: good and evil, beauty and ugliness,
     knowledge and innocence, spirit and matter, etc.;
4) The quaternity: the four elements, four-horse team, the
     axiom of Maria (3 + 1), etc.;
5) The coniunctio: Faust and Gretchen, Oberon and Titania's
     golden wedding, Faust and Helen.

These are also the central motifs of alchemy and of the process of
individuation. In particular Jung has singled out the coniunctio:

> [The main concern of alchemy is] the mystery of the *coniunctio,* or
> "chymical wedding," which runs through the whole of *Faust.* I have
> devoted a special work to this problem—*Mysterium Coniunctionis.*
> . . . It contains everything that forms the historical background—so
> far as this is alchemical—of *Faust.* These roots go very deep and
> seem to me to explain much of the numinous effect which emanates
> from Goethe's "main work."[1]

According to Jung[2] the forerunner of Goethe's *Faust* was *The*

---

[1] *Letters,* vol. 2, p. 246.

[2] "The Psychology of the Transference," *The Practice of Psychotherapy,* CW
16, par. 500

Chemical Wedding (1616) by Christian Rosencreutz, who also wrote a Faust drama. The hero of the latter is "a learned know-it-all who, disillusioned with the sciences, finally returns to Christianity."[3]

The Chemical Wedding is an alchemical allegory in which the protagonist, after a series of trials and ordeals which establish him as an elected one, is permitted to witness and participate in an elaborate procedure involving the death and regeneration of a royal couple. The process is very similar to that depicted by the *Rosarium* pictures,[4] with the additional feature that, as in *Faust*, the figure representing the ego intervenes in the coniunctio of the archetypal figures and suffers effects of that intervention. In *The Chemical Wedding* this happens when the protagonist slips into Venus' bedchamber and gazes on her naked beauty. He is later punished for this transgression by being sentenced to servitude as gate keeper of the coniunctio castle. This work, notes Jung, was "assuredly known to Goethe."[5]

In *Faust*, the product of the coniunctio is lost four times: 1) Gretchen murders her baby; 2) Boy Charioteer disappears in the flaming conclusion of the pageant; 3) Homunculus crashes in flames onto Galatea's throne; 4) Euphorion falls to his death. Evidently Goethe was able only to anticipate the coniunctio but not to achieve it. In a letter written to someone who did not appreciate the reality of Faust, Jung says,

> Obviously the processes in Faust are real. Such things cannot possibly be "wishful fantasies." They are on the contrary the material which, when it comes up in a man, can make him go mad. This is also true of the fourth stage of the transformation process;[6] the experience in the Beyond. It is an unconscious reality which in Faust's case was felt as being beyond his reach at the time, and for this reason it is separated from his real existence by death. It expresses the

---

[3] *The Symbolic Life,* CW 18, par. 1692.

[4] See Jung, "The Psychology of the Transference," *The Practice of Psychotherapy,* CW 16.

[5] Ibid., par. 407.

[6] The fourth transformation of Faust—into Doctor Marianus—after his mysterious death (Part II, act 5, last scene).

fact that he still had to "become a boy" and only then would he attain the highest wisdom. Euphorion stands for the future man who does not flee from the bond with the earth but is dashed to pieces on it, which means that he is not viable under the existing circumstances. Faust's death must therefore be taken as a fact. But like many a death it is really a mystery death which brings the imperfect to perfection.

The Paris-Helen-Euphorion episode is actually the highest stage that the transformation process has reached, but not in itself the highest, for the element Euphorion has not been integrated into the Faust-Mephisto-Paris-Helen quaternity as the *quinta essentia.*[7]

The Faust drama demonstrates that individuation is accompanied by guilt.[8] The danger is that when the guilt reaches consciousness it may overwhelm the ego with a sense of its own evil (negative inflation), a condition symbolized by the image "damnation to hell." Faust is spared that fate by the loving assistance of the Gretchen anima in heaven. In other words Faust's redemption is the result of an unconscious process. From the vantage point of depth psychology we can see how that process can be made conscious. The play begins with the "Prologue in Heaven," in which we learn that the whole drama is initiated by a divine wager between Mephistopheles and the Lord. This means that Faust's struggle for fulfillment originates in the Self, the transpersonal psyche. Thus the guilt incurred by the ego is shared by the Self. It is a necessary consequence of the process of coming to consciousness. In that process God (the Lord plus Mephistopheles) reveals his own nature and undergoes transformation through being seen.[9]

Faust was Jung's "heritage."[10] For all who claim to be Jungian, it will also be theirs. With all its darkness and ambiguity it is a "Jungian" story which passes on to all Jungians the task of repenting Faust's guilt and of rebuilding the shrine of Baucis and Philemon.

---

[7] *Letters,* vol. 1, pp. 264f.
[8] "Life itself is guilt." (Jung, *Mysterium Coniunctionis,* CW 14, par. 206)
[9] See Edinger, *The Creation of Consciousness,* pp. 52ff, 91ff.
[10] *Letters,* vol. 1, pp. 309f.

From Thomas Aquinas (pseud.), "De Alchimia" (16th cent.).

Appendix
Helen of Troy[*]

Eris, the goddess of discord, started it by throwing into the midst of the assembled gods a golden apple inscribed "for the fairest." Hera, Athena and Aphrodite each claimed the apple was rightfully hers. Zeus decreed that the shepherd, Paris, must decide the dispute among the goddesses and sent Hermes to lead them to Paris. Each goddess offered Paris a bribe if he would choose her. Hera promised dominion of the earth. Athena, wisdom and victories in battle. Aphrodite offered him Helen, the most beautiful woman in the world. Paris decided in favor of Aphrodite and she helped him to abduct Helen from her husband, Menelaus. To recover Helen, the Greeks attacked Troy. Thus began the Trojan War.

The judgment of Paris was a cruel task to impose on an innocent shepherd boy, yet this story pictures an archetypal stage of development in the life of everyone. Each of us must decide what he will put first: Hera, Athena or Aphrodite, that is, power, knowledge or love. Whichever the choice, one is then projected into the war of life. And, sooner or later, the goddesses who have been rejected will return to insist on their due. Paris chose Aphrodite first and his reward was Helen. Others make other first choices and order their lives around power or knowledge. But if one is to be whole, eventually Aphrodite and her handmaiden, Helen of Troy, must be given priority.

The alchemists used the judgment of Paris as an analogy of one stage of the alchemical opus. The picture opposite shows Paris waking a sleeping king as he makes his decision.[1] Thus the larger

---

[*] Originally published in *A Well of Living Waters,* a Festschrift for Hilde Kirsch, C.G. Jung Institute of Los Angeles, 1977.

[1] Reprinted from Jung, *Psychology and Alchemy,* CW 12, fig. 9.

personality, the inner authority, is brought into effective operation by making the crucial judgment.

Helen is perhaps the most impressive and enduring image in Western culture of the power of the feminine to lure men into life. Gilbert Murray describes the image of Helen in these words, written in 1907, before the concept of the collective unconscious had been developed:

> Think how the beauty of Helen has lived through the ages . . . it is now an immortal thing. And the main, though not of course the sole, source of the whole conception is certainly the *Iliad*. Yet in the whole *Iliad* there is practically not a word spoken in description of Helen . . . almost the whole of our knowledge of Helen's beauty comes from a few lines in the third book, where Helen goes up to the wall of Troy to see the battle between Menelaus and Paris. "So speaking, the goddess put into her heart a longing for her husband of yore and her city and her father and mother. And straightaway she veiled herself with white linen, and went forth from her chamber shedding a great tear . . ." The elders of Troy were seated on the wall, and when they saw Helen coming, "softly they spake to one another winged words: 'Small wonder that the Trojans and mailed Greeks should endure pain through many years for such a woman. *Strangely like she is in face of some immortal spirit'.*" That is all we know. Not one of all the Homeric bards fell into the yawning trap of describing Helen, and making a catalogue of her features. She was veiled; she was weeping; and she was strangely like in face to some immortal spirit. And the old men, who strove for peace, could feel no anger at the war.[2]
>
> [Images like] the weeping face of Helen . . . have behind them not the imagination of one great poet, but the accumulated emotion, one may almost say, of the many successive generations who have heard and learned and themselves afresh re-created the old majesty and loveliness. They are like watchwords of great causes for which men have fought and died; charged with power from the first to attract men's love, but now through the infinite shining back of that love, grown to yet greater power. There is in them, as it were, the spiritual life-blood of a people.[3]

---

[2] *The Rise of the Greek Epic*, p. 224.
[3] Ibid., p. 231.

Helen of Troy is indeed an "immortal spirit" who is "charged with power to attract men's love." In other words, she is an image of an aspect of the archetypal feminine. In the original myth she is the bait that lures Paris into independent functioning. By daring to make a judgment he becomes an autonomous center of being, i.e., an ego. The Gospel says, "Judge not, that ye be not judged,"[4] but egohood requires taking on oneself the hybris of judgment. By making choices man senses that he is stumbling, like Laocoön, into the serpentine coils of a tragic process. He would prefer not to get involved. (Paris first suggested he divide the apple equally among the goddesses.) He must be seduced into becoming an individual.

Helen appears in a new context in the myth of Simon Magus the Gnostic. She was the companion of Simon's work and travels and had been found by him in a brothel in Tyre. Helen was identified with the fallen Sophia, Wisdom of God, whom Simon had come to redeem.[5] It was said of this Gnostic Helen that she was

> brought down from the higher heavens . . . Wisdom, the mother of all things for whom . . . the Greeks and barbarians contending were able in some measure to see an image of her; but of herself, as she is, as the dweller with the first and only God, they were totally ignorant.[6]

In the Gnostic myth, Helen has been recast in a drama concerning redemption of the soul. Another phase of psychic development is now pictured. The soul, after luring the ego into life (coagulatio),[7] has herself fallen into the captive embrace of matter. She must now be redeemed from the literal, the concrete and the particular in order to be recognized in her full magnitude as a transpersonal power (sublimatio).[8] Helen's rescue by Simon and her recognition as the fallen Wisdom of God corresponds to the teaching Socrates received

---

[4] Matt. 7:1.
[5] See Hans Jonas, *The Gnostic Religion,* p. 104.
[6] *Clementine Recognitions* II, 12. *Ante-Nicene Fathers* VIII, 100.
[7] See Edinger, *Anatomy of the Psyche,* chapter 4.
[8] Ibid., chapter 5.

from the wise Diotima, whereby he moved from the love of beautiful bodies to the love of beautiful souls and finally to the numinous vision of Love and Beauty themselves.[9]

Simon Magus was the prototype for the legend of Faust. Thus Helen appears in the Faust stories of both Marlowe and Goethe as the goal of the quest. Her beauty and promise of life-renewal lure Faust into his historic encounter with the power of darkness. When Helen enters, Marlowe's Doctor Faustus expresses her numinosity in these beautiful lines:

> Was this the face that launched a thousand ships
> And burnt the topless towers of Ilium?
> Sweet Helen, make me immortal with a kiss.
> Her lips suck forth my soul. See where it flies!
> Come Helen, come, give me my soul again.
> Here will I dwell, for heaven is in these lips
> And all is dross that is not Helena.
> I will be Paris, and for love of thee
> Instead of Troy shall Wittenberg be sacked;
> And I will combat with weak Menelaus
> And wear thy colors on my plumèd crest.
> Yea, I will wound Achilles in the heel
> And then return to Helen for a kiss.
> O, thou art fairer than the evening's air
> Clad in the beauty of a thousand stars,
> Brighter art thou than flaming Jupiter
> When he appeared to hapless Semele,
> More lovely than the monarch of the sky
> In wanton Arethusa's azure arms,
> And none but thou shalt be my paramour.[10]

These lines indicate that for Doctor Faustus, Helen is the *numinosum* itself. For him then to seek personal possession of her is very ominous. If Helen is brighter "than flaming Jupiter when he appeared to hapless Semele," then Faustus is risking the fate of Semele. Indeed, this is what happens. Helen had been summoned up for

---

[9] See Plato, *Symposium,* 201ff.

[10] Christopher Marlowe, *Dr. Faustus,* act. 5, scene 1, lines 96-115.

Faustus' personal pleasure. In his attempt to possess an archetypal energy, the ego falls into identification with the Self and is destroyed. *Doctor Faustus* ends with Faustus being dragged shrieking into hell. The final lines of the Chorus provide the moral.

> Cut is the branch that might have grown full straight
> And burned is Apollo's laurel bough
> That sometime grew within this learned man.
> Faustus is gone. Regard his hellish fall!
> —Whose fiendful fortune may exhort the wise
> Only to wonder at unlawful things
> Whose deepness doth entice such forward wits
> To practice more than heavenly power permits.[11]

Marlowe's Doctor Faustus is a case of arrested development. He follows his anima of desirousness until she leads him to hell (calcinatio),[12] and there the story ends. There is no transformation and no opening of the collective unconscious.

Goethe's *Faust* is different. Already in Faust's early conversation with Mephistopheles he reveals his difference from Marlowe's Faustus by asking his visitor not for power and pleasure, but for the full range of human feeling.

> Have you not heard?—I do not ask for joy.
> I take the way of turmoil's bitterest gain,
> Of love-sick hate, of quickening bought with pain.
> My heart, from learning's tyranny set free,
> Shall no more shun distress, but take its toll
> Of all the hazards of humanity,
> And nourish mortal sadness in my soul.
> I'll sound the heights and depths that men can know,
> Their very souls shall be with mine entwined,
> I'll load my bosom with their weal and woe,
> And share with them the shipwreck of mankind.[13]

Faust is lured into experiencing "the heights and depths that men

---

[11] Ibid., act 5, scene 3, lines 1ff.

[12] See Edinger, *Anatomy of the Psyche,* chapter 2.

[13] Part I, act 1, "Study," Wayne translation.

can know" by Mephistopheles who shows him the image of a ravish-
ingly beautiful woman. Faust exclaims:

> What do I see? What form divinely fair
> Within this magic mirror is revealed?
> Oh lend me, Love, they swiftest wing and bear
> Me hence into her wondrous field!
> The fairest image of a woman! Can it be,
> Is it possible? Can woman be so fair?
> Must I in that recumbent body there
> Behold of all the heavens the epitome?
> Can one so fair be found on earth?[14]

At the end of the scene, Faust implores,

> Let me but briefly gaze once more into the glass,
> Ah! too fair seemed that woman's-form![15]

And Mephistopheles replies,

> No, no! A model that no woman can surpass,
> You'll see anon alive and warm.
> With this drink in your body, soon you'll greet
> A Helena in every girl you meet.[16]

In Part II, Act 1, the images of Paris and Helen are brought up
from the depths by Faust's descent to "the Mothers." When Helen
appears, Faust is enraptured:

> Have I still eyes? Is Beauty's spring, outpouring,
> Revealed most richly to my inmost soul?
> My dread path brought me to this loftiest goal!
> Void was the world and barred to my exploring!
> What is it now since this my priesthood's hour?
> Worth wishing for, firm-based, a lasting dower!
> Vanish from me my every vital power
> If I forsake thee, treacherous to my duty!
> The lovely form that once my fancy captured,

---

14 Ibid., "Witch's Kitchen," Priest translation.
15 Ibid.
16 Ibid.

That in the magic glass enraptured,
Was but a foam-born phantom of such beauty!—
To thee alone I render up with gladness
The very essence of my passion,
Fancy, desire, love, worship, madness![17]

Faust cannot bear to watch the drama of Helen's abduction by Paris. He rashly seizes Helen out of Paris's grasp. The image of Helen vanishes and Faust falls unconscious.

In Part II, Act 3, the union of Faust with Helen comes closer to completion. Faust again seeks Helen and finds her in classical Greece. They unite and have a child, Euphorion. But again Helen fades away after the child tries to fly and falls to his death like Icarus.

Finally, at the death of Faust, his immortal part is saved and led to heaven in the company of a group of penitent women. Goethe concludes his great opus with these words:

O contrite hearts, seek with your eyes
The visage of salvation;
Blissful in that gaze, arise,
Through glad regeneration.
Now may every pulse of good
Seek to serve before thy face,
Virgin, Queen of Motherhood,
Keep us, Goddess, in thy grace.

All things corruptible
Are but a parable;
Earth's insufficiency
Here finds fulfillment;
Here the ineffable
Wins life through love;
Eternal Womanhood
Leads us above.[18]

This is the climax of the literary tradition. Helen of Troy, the seductress and cause of war and pillage, has become the eternal femi-

---

[17] Part II, act 1, Priest translation.
[18] Ibid., act 5, Wayne translation.

nine. It was left for Jung to establish the psychological meaning of this development as the evolution of the anima. He writes:

> Four stages [of erotic phenomenology] were known in the late classical period: Hawwah (Eve), Helen (of Troy), the Virgin Mary, and Sophia. The series is repeated in Goethe's *Faust:* in the figures of Gretchen as the personification of a purely instinctual relationship (Eve); Helen as an anima figure; Mary as the personification of the "heavenly," i.e., Christian or religious, relationship; and the "eternal feminine" as an expression of the alchemical *Sapientia.* As the nomenclature shows, we are dealing with the heterosexual Eros or anima-figure in four stages, and consequently with four stages of the Eros cult. The first stage—Hawwah, Eve, earth—is purely biological; woman is equated with the mother and only represents something to be fertilized. The second stage is still dominated by the sexual Eros, but on an aesthetic and romantic level where woman has already acquired some value as an individual. The third stage raises Eros to the heights of religious devotion and thus spiritualizes him: Hawwah has been replaced by spiritual motherhood. Finally, the fourth stage illustrates something which unexpectedly goes beyond the almost unsurpassable third stage: *Sapientia.* How can wisdom transcend the most holy and the most pure?—Presumably only by virtue of the truth that the less sometimes means the more. This stage represents spiritualization of Helen and consequently of Eros as such.[19]

The "spiritualization of Eros" is a symbolic phrase which will not yield a single, simple meaning. But surely it points to the redemption and transformation of the erotic when it functions not out of dissociation but out of wholeness. To bring this about is one of the tasks of our time.

---

[19] "The Psychology of the Transference," *The Practice of Psychotherapy,* CW 16, par. 361.

Bibliography

English translations of *Faust*

Arndt, Walter. *Goethe, Faust.* Ed. Cyrus Hamlin. Norton Critical Edition. Norton, New York, 1976.

Fairley, Barker. *Goethe's Faust.* University of Toronto Press, Buffalo, 1985.

Kaufmann. *Goethe's Faust.* Part I only. Anchor Books, Doubleday and Co., Garden City, NY, 1963.

Luke, David. *Goethe, Faust.* Part I only. Oxford University Press, New York, 1987.

MacNiece, Louis. *Goethe's Faust.* Abridged. Galaxy, Oxford University Press, New York, 1963.

Priest, George Madison. *Goethe, Faust.* Alfred A. Knopf, New York, 1963.

Raphael, Alice. *Goethe, Faust.* Part I only. Holt, Rinehart and Winston, New York, 1963.

Salm, Peter. *Goethe, Faust.* Part I only. Dual Language Bantam Books, New York, 1985.

Taylor, Bayard. *Goethe, Faust.* Random House Modern Library, New York, n.d.

Wayne, Philip. *Goethe, Faust.* 2 vols. Penguin Books, Baltimore, 1969.

General

Ante-Nicene Fathers. 10 vols. Ed. Roberts and Donaldson. Eerdmans, Grand Rapids, MI, reprinted 1977.

Apollodorus. Trans. J.G. Frazer. 2 vols. Loeb Classical Library, Harvard University Press, Cambridge, MA, 1963.

Burkert, Walter. *Lore and Science in Ancient Pythagoreanism.* Harvard University Press, Cambridge, MA, 1972.

Burnet, John. *Early Greek Philosophy.* Meridian Books, World Publishing Co., New York, 1962.

Butler, E. M. *The Fortunes of Faust.* Cambridge University Press, Cambridge, 1979.

_____. *The Myth of the Magus.* Cambridge University Press, The MacMillan Co., New York, 1948.

Carlyle, Thomas. *Sartor Resartus.* Everyman's Library, Dent and Sons, London, 1948.

Edinger, Edward F. *Anatomy of the Psyche: Alchemical Symbolism in Psychotherapy.* Open Court, La Salle, IL, 1985.

_____. *The Bible and the Psyche: Individuation Symbolism in the Old Testament.* Inner City Books, Toronto, 1986.

_____. *The Creation of Consciousness: Jung's Myth for Modern Man.* Inner City Books, Toronto, 1984.

_____. *Ego and Archetype: Individuation and the Religious Function of the Psyche..* G. P. Putnam's Sons, New York, 1972.

_____. *Encounter with the Self: A Jungian Commentary on William Blake's Illustrations of the Book of Job.* Inner City Books, Toronto, 1986.

The Golden Legend of Jacobus de Voragine. Longmans, Green and Co., New York, 1948.

Gounod. *Faust.* Opera in Five Acts. Music by Charles Gounod. Libretto by Jules Barbier and Michel Carré. English translation of libretto accompanying RCA Red Seal Recording. RCA, New York, 1977.

Hall, James. *Dictionary of Subjects and Symbols in Art.* Harper and Row, New York, 1979.

The Hermetic Museum. 2 vols. Trans. A. E. Waite. John M. Watkins, London, 1953.

Jaffé, Aniela, ed. *C.G. Jung: Word and Image* (Bollingen Series XCVII:2). Princeton University Press, Princeton, 1979.

Jonas, Hans. *The Gnostic Religion.* Beacon Press, Boston, 1958.

Jung, C.G. *The Collected Works* (Bollingen Series XX). 20 vols. Trans. R.F.C. Hull. Ed. H. Read, M. Fordham, G. Adler, Wm. McGuire. Princeton University Press, Princeton, 1953-1979.

_____. *Letters* (Bollingen Series XCV). 2 vols. Princeton University Press, Princeton, 1973.

_____. *Memories, Dreams, Reflections.* Pantheon Books, New York, 1961.

_____. *Nietzsche's Zarathustra: Notes of the Seminar Given in 1934-1939* (Bollingen Series XCIX). 2 vols. Ed. James L. Jarrett. Princeton University Press, Princeton, 1988.

_____. *Interpretation of Visions: Notes on Seminar Given in Zurich, 1930-34.* 11 vols. Mimeographed.

Jung, Emma, and von Franz, Marie-Louise. *The Grail Legend.* 2nd ed. Trans. Andrea Dykes. Sigo Press, Boston, 1986.

Keats, John. *The Poems of John Keats.* Oxford University Press, London, 1961.

Kirk, G.S., and Raven, J.E. *The Presocratic Philosophers.* Cambridge University Press, Cambridge, 1963.

Marlowe, Christopher. *Doctor Faustus.* New American Library, Signet, New York, 1969.

Mary Knoll Missal. P. J. Kennedy and Sons, New York, 1960.

Milton, John. *Complete Poetry and Selected Prose.* Nonesuch Library, University Press, Glasgow, 1969.

Murray, Gilbert. *The Rise of the Greek Epic.* Clarendon Press, Oxford, 1907.

Plato. *Symposium.* Loeb Classical Library, Harvard University Press, Cambridge, MA, 1953.

Rilke, Rainer Maria. *Poems from the Book of Hours.* Trans. Babette Deutsche. New Directions, New York, 1975.

_____. *The Duino Elegies,* in *The Selected Poetry of R.M. Rilke.* Trans. Stephen Mitchell. Vintage Books, Random House, New York, 1984.

Virgil. *Georgics,* vol. 1. Loeb Classical Library, Harvard University Press, Cambridge, MA, 1978.

A Well of Living Waters. Festschrift for Hilde Kirsch. C.G. Jung Institute of Los Angeles, 1977.

Wilke, H.-J. *"Faust und die Sorge Anmerkungen zur Ueberwindung des Heroischen." Analytische Psychologie,* vol. 20, no. 1 (1989).

Yeats, W.B. *The Collected Poems of W. B. Yeats.* Macmillan, New York, 1970.

Index

active imagination, 16, 28-29
Adler, Alfred, 79
Aegean Festival, 66-69
Aion (Jung), 13
alchemy/alchemists, 20, 25-26, 33, 35,
  38, 41, 49, 61, 67-68, 74, 89,
  92-93, 96-97, 104
amor fati, 86
angel, struggle with, 28-29
anima *(see also* Helen), 35, 38, 44-45,
  47, 83, 94, 101, 104
anima christiana, 13
Annunciation, 65
Antichrist, 13-14, 23
Aphrodite, 79, 97
Apocalypse, 13
Aquinas, Thomas, 96
Arcadia, 72-73
archetypal pattern(s), 40-41, 45, 73-75,
  97-99
Ares, 79
Arisleus, 46-47
asceticism, 25, 28
astrology, 13
Athena, 97
Auerbach's Tavern, 34-36, 40, 45, 51,
  69
Auseinandersetzung, 69
autonomous psyche, 16, 62
Axiom of Maria Prophetissa, 38, 92

Baucis, 81-83, 94
Beya, 46-47
"Book of Lambspring, The," 35
Boy Charioteer, 52-53, 93
Burial Mass, 41-42
Butler, E.M., 14

calcinatio, 101
calf, golden, 50-51
"Cantilena," 46
Care, 82-83
Carlyle, Thomas, 29

Carnival, 51-52
Carpocrates, doctrine of, 25n
Castor, 65
Cerberus, 26
chaos, 25, 33
Chemical Wedding, The, 92-93
Chymical Wedding, The, 67
Christ, 13-14, 23, 33, 76-80
Christian/Christianity, 13-14, 23, 25-
  26, 28, 32-33, 41-42, 45, 51-52,
  65, 78, 90, 93
Clytemnestra, 65
coagulatio, 99
collective unconscious, 63, 69, 98, 101
Columbus, Christopher, 13
Communion, 36
compensation, 14, 33
conception, psychic, 61
conflict, 15, 25, 48, 78-81
coniunctio, 41-45, 47, 53, 54n, 56, 59,
  61, 65, 67-70, 73-74, 79, 86, 90,
  92-94
Copernicus, 13
Corregio, 65
cup, 41-42

da Vinci, Leonardo, 13, 65
Danäe, 65
Delphic Oracle, 57
depression, 20
Devil: in Christianity, 32
  as dynamic aspect of Lord, 18
  pact with, 32
"Dies Irae," 41-42
Dionysus, 32, 36, 51-52
divine child, 73
divinity, experience of, 28-29
dog, black, 21, 23-28
Doctor Faustus (Marlowe), 43, 100-101
dragon, 35

Earth-spirit, 21
Easter, 23

Studies in Jungian Psychology
by Jungian Analysts

Quality Paperbacks

Prices and payment in $US (in Canada, $Cdn)

The Mysterium Lectures: A Journey through Jung's *Mysterium Coniunctionis*
Edward F. Edinger (Los Angeles) ISBN 0-919123-66-X. 90 illustrations. 352 pp. $20

The Creation of Consciousness: Jung's Myth for Modern Man
Edward F. Edinger (Los Angeles) ISBN 0-919123-13-9. Illustrated. 128 pp. $15

The Mystery of the Coniunctio: Alchemical Image of Individuation
Edward F. Edinger (Los Angeles) ISBN 0-919123-67-8. Illustrated. 112pp. $14

Conscious Femininity: Interviews with Marion Woodman
Introduction by Marion Woodman (Toronto) ISBN 0-919123-59-7. 160 pp. $16

The Middle Passage: From Misery to Meaning in Midlife
James Hollis (Philadelphia) ISBN 0-919123-60-0. 128 pp. $15

Eros and Pathos: Shades of Love and Suffering
Aldo Carotenuto (Rome) ISBN 0-919123-39-2. 144 pp. $16

Descent to the Goddess: A Way of Initiation for Women
Sylvia Brinton Perera (New York) ISBN 0-919123-05-8. 112 pp. $15

Addiction to Perfection: The Still Unravished Bride
Marion Woodman (Toronto) ISBN 0-919123-11-2. Illustrated. 208 pp. $18pb/$20hc

The Illness That We Are: A Jungian Critique of Christianity
John P. Dourley (Ottawa) ISBN 0-919123-16-3. 128 pp. $15

Coming To Age: The Croning Years and Late-Life Transformation
Jane R. Prétat (Providence) ISBN 0-919123-63-5. 144 pp. $16

The Jungian Experience: Analysis and Individuation
James A. Hall, M.D. (Dallas) ISBN 0-919123-25-2. 176 pp. $18

Phallos: Sacred Image of the Masculine
Eugene Monick (Scranton) ISBN 0-919123-26-0. 30 illustrations. 144 pp. $16

Personality Types: Jung's Model of Typology
Daryl Sharp (Toronto) ISBN 0-919123-30-9. Diagrams. 128 pp. $15

The Sacred Prostitute: Eternal Aspect of the Feminine
Nancy Qualls-Corbett (Birmingham) ISBN 0-919123-31-7. Illustrated. 176 pp. $18

Close Relationships: Family, Friendship, Marriage
Eleanor Bertine (New York) ISBN 0-919123-46-5. 160 pp. $16

Under Saturn's Shadow: The Wounding and Healing of Men
James Hollis (Philadelphia) ISBN 0-919123-64-3. 144 pp. $16

Jung Lexicon: A Primer of Terms & Concepts
Daryl Sharp (Toronto) ISBN 0-919123-48-1. Diagrams. 160 pp. $16

Discounts: any 3-5 books, 10%; 6 books or more, 20%
Add Postage/Handling: 1-2 books, $2; 3-4 books, $4; 5-9 books, $8; 10 or more, free

Write or phone for free Catalogue of 70+ titles

INNER CITY BOOKS
Box 1271, Station Q, Toronto, ON M4T 2P4, Canada   (416) 927-0355